2017-2018 Supplement

National Security Law
Sixth Edition

and

Counterterrorism Law
Third Edition

ASPEN CASEBOOK SERIES

2017–2018 Supplement

National Security Law
Sixth Edition

and

Counterterrorism Law
Third Edition

Stephen Dycus
Professor of Law
Vermont Law School

William C. Banks
Board of Advisors Distinguished Professor
Syracuse University College of Law

Peter Raven-Hansen
Glen Earl Weston Research Professor of Law Emeritus
George Washington University

Stephen I. Vladeck
Professor of Law
University of Texas School of Law

Wolters Kluwer

About Wolters Kluwer Legal & Regulatory U.S.

Wolters Kluwer Legal & Regulatory U.S. delivers expert content and solutions in the areas of law, corporate compliance, health compliance, reimbursement, and legal education. Its practical solutions help customers successfully navigate the demands of a changing environment to drive their daily activities, enhance decision quality and inspire confident outcomes.

Serving customers worldwide, its legal and regulatory portfolio includes products under the Aspen Publishers, CCH Incorporated, Kluwer Law International, ftwilliam.com and MediRegs names. They are regarded as exceptional and trusted resources for general legal and practice-specific knowledge, compliance and risk management, dynamic workflow solutions, and expert commentary.

Contents

Contents

Contents

Preface

When we published the latest editions of *National Security Law* and *Counterterrorism Law* last summer, we harbored no illusion as to the need to continue our regular updates of fields that, in recent years, have produced a simply stunning flood of important and momentous legal, policy, and political developments. But even with those expectations, staying abreast of the relevant changes over the past year has felt, at times, like trying to drink from a fire hose. The 126 pages of material in this year's *Supplement* reflect our best effort to keep both casebooks as current as practicable under the circumstances without overloading adopters and students with more material than could (or should) reasonably be encompassed within the relevant coursework.

Some of this year's additions to the *Supplement* will already be familiar to many readers — including detailed materials on the ongoing litigation challenging President Trump's "Travel Ban"; discussions of key interpretations of (and tweaks to) government surveillance authorities in advance of the debate over reauthorization of Section 702 of the Foreign Intelligence Surveillance Act; and updates on key court rulings on topics ranging from *"Bivens"* remedies and whether the 2001 Authorization for the Use of Military Force applies to the Islamic State in Iraq and Syria to the Guantánamo military commissions and a major test-case for the future of the third-party doctrine in Fourth Amendment jurisprudence.

But we have also endeavored to include other materials that add depth and richness to the latest editions of our casebooks, even though they have not generated as many headlines — including subtle but significant developments with respect to the use of military force overseas (and congressional oversight thereof here at home); Congress's enactment, over President Obama's veto, of the Justice Against Sponsors of Terrorism Act; and recent amendments to the Federal Records Act and Presidential Records Act that could have significant ramifications for President Trump's use of Twitter. As even a cursory perusal of the *Supplement*'s Table of Contents indicates, this year may not have had the same *number* of national security headlines as other recent years, but it was hardly lacking in meaningful legal developments. By way of comparison, this *Supplement* is twice as long as the version we produced the first year after the last editions of the casebooks were published.

This *Supplement* serves two closely related casebooks: *National Security Law* (6th ed.) and *Counterterrorism Law* (3d ed.). This Preface is followed immediately by two Teacher's Guides, one for each book, which indicate the placement of supplemental materials within each casebook (and should therefore make it easier for adopters to match *Supplement* entries to their syllabi). Each document listed is accompanied by a reference to one or both casebooks. For example, the new materials on the Travel Ban litigation (*Supplement* p. 49) appear with this instruction: **[NSL p. 826, CTL p. 454. Insert after Note 4.]** "NSL" refers to *National Security Law* (6th ed.), and "CTL" to *Counterterrorism Law* (3d ed.). Some of the instructions, like the above example, suggest that the *Supplement* materials should be provided in addition to the relevant casebook pages; others suggest replacing what's in the casebook with these more recent discussions — which, in many cases, provide more concise, more relevant, or, at the very least, more definitive discussions of the topics raised in the original casebook materials. In all cases, our hope is that, as a result of this *Supplement*, you'll find our materials not just to be pedagogically valuable in the abstract, but also *current* — an invaluable commodity in a field that is expanding in hitherto unexplored directions every month (if not more often).

Finally, as important new developments arise during the coming year, we will continue to document them by posting edited new materials on the websites for the two casebooks — supplements to this *Supplement* — from which they may be downloaded by teachers and shared with students. The website for *National Security Law* (6th ed.) may be found at http://www.aspenlawschool.com/books/Dycus_NatSec/default.asp; the website for *Counterterrorism Law* (3d ed.) may be found at http://www.aspenlawschool.com/books/Dycus_CounterTerror/default.asp. We encourage you to return to those portals to keep abreast of major developments during the year — and to let us know if and when you come across new materials that deserve to be included.

As always, we are extremely grateful to our adopters, fellow members of the National Security Law Section of the Association of American Law Schools, fellow members of the Editorial Board of the *Journal of National Security Law & Policy*, fellow casebook authors (our collaborators in building the field), members of the ABA Standing Committee on Law and National Security, and our many friends in the national security community. We also wish to thank our research assistants. Finally, we wish to express our gratitude to John Devins and Carol McGeehan, our long-time editors and friends, for their longstanding encouragement and support, and to Patrick Cline, Lori Wood, and Troy Froebe for their excellent editorial support in the completion of this latest *Supplement*.

Stephen Dycus
William C. Banks
Peter Raven-Hansen
Stephen I. Vladeck

July 2017

Teacher's Guide for National Security Law (6th Edition)

Chapter 13. Unilateral Use of Force

Chapter 14. Targeting Terrorists

Chapter 15. Cyber Operations

Chapter 18. Organization of and Authority for the Intelligence Community

Chapter 21. The Fourth Amendment and National Security

Chapter 22. Congressional Authority for Foreign Intelligence Surveillance

Chapter 23. Programmatic Electronic Foreign Intelligence Surveillance

Chapter 24. Third-Party Records — Targeted Collection

Chapter 25. Bulk Collection and Data Mining

Chapter 26. Screening for Security

Chapter 28. Habeas Corpus:
The Scope of the Suspension Clause

Chapter 30. Military Detention of Non-U.S. Persons

Chapter 31. Preventive Detention

Chapter 32. Interrogating Terrorist Suspects

Chapter 33. Case Study of Coercive Interrogation
of Detainees in U.S. Custody After 9/11

Chapter 34. Criminalizing Terrorism
and Material Support

Chapter 37. *Trial by Military Commission*

Chapter 38. *Homeland Security*

Chapter 41. *Statutory Access to National Security Information*

Chapter 42. *Other Grounds for Access to National Security Information*

Chapter 43. *Restraining Unauthorized Disclosures*

Teacher's Guide for Counterterrorism Law (3rd Edition)

Chapter 7. The Fourth Amendment and Counterterrorism

Chapter 8. Congressional Authority for Foreign Intelligence Surveillance

Chapter 9. Programmatic Electronic Foreign Intelligence Surveillance

Chapter 10. Third-Party Records — Targeted Collection

Chapter 11. Bulk Collection and Data Mining

Chapter 12. Screening for Security

Chapter 14. Habeas Corpus: The Scope of the Suspension Clause

Chapter 16. Military Detention of Non-U.S. Persons

Chapter 17. Preventive Detention

Chapter 18. Interrogating Terrorist Suspects

Chapter 19. Case Study of Coercive Interrogation of Detainees in U.S. Custody After 9/11

Table of Cases

Washington v. Trump
United States Court of Appeals, Ninth Circuit (Feb. 9, 2017)
847 F.3d 1151

Before: WILLIAM C. CANBY, RICHARD R. CLIFTON, and MICHELLE T. FRIEDLAND, Circuit Judges

PER CURIAM: At issue in this emergency proceeding is Executive Order 13769, "Protecting the Nation From Foreign Terrorist Entry Into the United States," which, among other changes to immigration policies and procedures, bans for 90 days the entry into the United States of individuals from seven countries. Two States challenged the Executive Order as unconstitutional and violative of federal law, and a federal district court preliminarily ruled in their favor and temporarily enjoined enforcement of the Executive Order. The Government now moves for an emergency stay of the district court's temporary restraining order while its appeal of that order proceeds. . . .

IV. Reviewability of the Executive Order

The Government contends that the district court lacked authority to enjoin enforcement of the Executive Order because the President has "unreviewable authority to suspend the admission of any class of aliens." The Government does not merely argue that courts owe substantial deference to the immigration and national security policy determinations of the political branches — an uncontroversial principle that is well-grounded in our jurisprudence. *See, e.g., Cardenas v. United States*, 826 F.3d 1164, 1169 (9th Cir. 2016) (recognizing that "the power to expel or exclude aliens [is] a fundamental sovereign attribute exercised by the Government's political departments largely immune from judicial control" (quoting *Fiallo v. Bell*, 430 U.S. 787, 792 (1977))); *see also Holder v. Humanitarian Law Project*, 561 U.S. 1, 33-34 (2010) (explaining that courts should defer to the political branches with respect to national security and foreign relations). Instead, the Government has taken the position that the President's decisions about immigration policy, particularly when motivated by national security concerns, are *unreviewable*, even if those actions potentially contravene constitutional rights and protections. The Government indeed asserts that it violates

1

separation of powers for the judiciary to entertain a constitutional challenge to executive actions such as this one.

There is no precedent to support this claimed unreviewability, which runs contrary to the fundamental structure of our constitutional democracy. *See Boumediene v. Bush*, 553 U.S. 723, 765 (2008) (rejecting the idea that, even by congressional statute, Congress and the Executive could eliminate federal court habeas jurisdiction over enemy combatants, because the "political branches" lack "the power to switch the Constitution on or off at will"). Within our system, it is the role of the judiciary to interpret the law, a duty that will sometimes require the "[r]esolution of litigation challenging the constitutional authority of one of the three branches." *Zivotofsky ex rel. Zivotofsky v. Clinton*, 566 U.S. 189, 196 (2012) (quoting *INS v. Chadha*, 462 U.S. 919, 943 (1983)). We are called upon to perform that duty in this case.

Although our jurisprudence has long counseled deference to the political branches on matters of immigration and national security, neither the Supreme Court nor our court has ever held that courts lack the authority to review executive action in those arenas for compliance with the Constitution. To the contrary, the Supreme Court has repeatedly and explicitly rejected the notion that the political branches have unreviewable authority over immigration or are not subject to the Constitution when policymaking in that context. *See Zadvydas v. Davis*, 533 U.S. 678, 695 (2001) (emphasizing that the power of the political branches over immigration "is subject to important constitutional limitations"); *Chadha*, 462 U.S. at 940-41 (rejecting the argument that Congress has "unreviewable authority over the regulation of aliens," and affirming that courts can review "whether Congress has chosen a constitutionally permissible means of implementing that power"). Our court has likewise made clear that "[a]lthough alienage classifications are closely connected to matters of foreign policy and national security," courts "can and do review foreign policy arguments that are offered to justify legislative or executive action when constitutional rights are at stake." *American-Arab Anti-Discrimination Comm. v. Reno*, 70 F.3d 1045, 1056 (9th Cir. 1995).

Kleindienst v. Mandel, 408 U.S. 753 (1972), does not compel a different conclusion. The Government cites *Mandel* for the proposition that "'when the Executive exercises' immigration authority 'on the basis of a facially legitimate and bona fide reason, the courts will [not] look behind the exercise of that discretion.'" The Government omits portions of the quoted language to imply that this standard governs judicial review of *all* executive exercises of immigration authority. In fact, the

Mandel standard applies to lawsuits challenging an executive branch official's decision to issue or deny an individual visa based on the application of a congressionally enumerated standard to the particular facts presented by that visa application. The present case, by contrast, is not about the application of a specifically enumerated congressional policy to the particular facts presented in an individual visa application. Rather, the States are challenging the President's *promulgation* of sweeping immigration policy. Such exercises of policymaking authority at the highest levels of the political branches are plainly not subject to the *Mandel* standard; as cases like *Zadvydas* and *Chadha* make clear, courts can and do review constitutional challenges to the substance and implementation of immigration policy. *See Zadvydas*, 533 U.S. at 695; *Chadha*, 462 U.S. at 940-41.

This is no less true when the challenged immigration action implicates national security concerns. *See Ex parte Quirin*, 317 U.S. 1, 19 (1942) (stating that courts have a duty, "in time of war as well as in time of peace, to preserve unimpaired the constitutional safeguards of civil liberty"); *Ex parte Milligan*, 71 U.S. (4 Wall.) 2, 120-21 (1866) ("The Constitution of the United States is a law for rulers and people, equally in war and in peace . . . under all circumstances."). We are mindful that deference to the political branches is particularly appropriate with respect to national security and foreign affairs, given the relative institutional capacity, informational access, and expertise of the courts. *See Humanitarian Law Project*, 561 U.S. at 33-34.

Nonetheless, "courts are not powerless to review the political branches' actions" with respect to matters of national security. *Alperin v. Vatican Bank*, 410 F.3d 532, 559 n.17 (9th Cir. 2005). To the contrary, while counseling deference to the national security determinations of the political branches, the Supreme Court has made clear that the Government's "authority and expertise in [such] matters do not automatically trump the Court's own obligation to secure the protection that the Constitution grants to individuals," even in times of war. *Humanitarian Law Project*, 561 U.S. at 34 (quoting *id.* at 61 (Breyer, J., dissenting)); *see also United States v. Robel*, 389 U.S. 258, 264 (1967) ("'[N]ational defense' cannot be deemed an end in itself, justifying any exercise of legislative power designed to promote such a goal. . . . It would indeed be ironic if, in the name of national defense, we would sanction the subversion of one of those liberties . . . which makes the defense of the Nation worthwhile."); *Zemel v. Rusk*, 381 U.S. 1, 17 (1965) ("[S]imply because a statute deals with foreign relations [does not mean that] it can grant the Executive totally unrestricted freedom of choice.").

Indeed, federal courts routinely review the constitutionality of — and even invalidate — actions taken by the executive to promote national security, and have done so even in times of conflict. *See, e.g., Boumediene*, 553 U.S. 723 (striking down a federal statute purporting to deprive federal courts of jurisdiction over habeas petitions filed by non-citizens being held as "enemy combatants" after being captured in Afghanistan or elsewhere and accused of authorizing, planning, committing, or aiding the terrorist attacks perpetrated on September 11, 2001); *Aptheker v. Sec'y of State*, 378 U.S. 500 (1964) (holding unconstitutional a statute denying passports to American members of the Communist Party despite national security concerns); *Ex parte Endo*, 323 U.S. 283 (1944) (holding unconstitutional the detention of a law-abiding and loyal American of Japanese ancestry during World War II and affirming federal court jurisdiction over habeas petitions by such individuals). As a plurality of the Supreme Court cautioned in *Hamdi v. Rumsfeld*, 542 U.S. 507 (2004), "Whatever power the United States Constitution envisions for the Executive in its exchanges with other nations or with enemy organizations in times of conflict, it most assuredly envisions a role for all three branches when individual liberties are at stake." *Id.* at 536 (plurality opinion).

In short, although courts owe considerable deference to the President's policy determinations with respect to immigration and national security, it is beyond question that the federal judiciary retains the authority to adjudicate constitutional challenges to executive action. . . .

[The court then proceeded to deny the government's emergency motion for a stay pending appeal of the lower court's order halting enforcement of the executive order on immigration.]

[NSL p. 144. Insert new Note.]

8. *Targeted Killings as Political Questions?* In *bin Ali Jaber v. United States*, No. 16-5093, 2017 WL 2818645 (D.C. Cir. June 30, 2017), the Court of Appeals held that claims brought on behalf of civilian victims who were collateral damage to a U.S. drone strike in Yemen posed non-justiciable political questions. It declared that "it is not the role of the Judiciary to second-guess the determination of the Executive, in coordination with the Legislature, that the interests of the

U.S. call for a particular military action in the ongoing War on Terror." *Id.* at *4. The court distinguished other cases in which federal courts *have* reviewed the validity of U.S. actions against terrorism suspects in the conflict with Al Qaeda, noting that those cases were justiciable "because the Constitution specifically contemplates a judicial role in this area," *id.* (citation omitted), even though the plaintiffs sued under a pair of statutes — the Alien Tort Statute, 28 U.S.C. §1350 (2012), and the Torture Victim Protection Act, 28 U.S.C. §1350 note (2012) — that expressly authorize private civil claims.

Note that this view would render non-justiciable virtually any civil lawsuit arising out of a drone strike (or other use of military force) carried out as part of the conflict with Al Qaeda — even where the use of force is wholly lacking factual or legal justification. Do you agree with such a sweeping rejection of a judicial role?

Regardless of how you answer that question, observe two oddities about the reasoning in *bin Ali Jaber*: First, the Court of Appeals never actually identified a specific "textually demonstrable commitment" or "lack of judicially manageable standards" that justified invocation of the political question doctrine; it merely relied on prior circuit precedent (which had also muddied the doctrinal inquiry). *See id.* at *4-5 (citing *El-Shifa Pharm. Indus. Co. v. United States*, 607 F.3d 836 (D.C. Cir. 2010) (en banc)).

Second, as we will see in Chapter 37, Congress has given the D.C. Circuit full appellate authority over the military tribunals at Guantánamo — in which the court has had to answer comparable factual and legal questions arising out of military operations against Al Qaeda and its affiliates. If Article III courts have the competence to answer those questions in reviewing decisions by military commissions, why does (and should) it make a difference if the very same questions arise in ordinary civil suits instead? Does it matter that, in the former cases, military authorities had a first crack at an adjudicative determination and that a reviewing court, therefore, is not conducting an unfiltered review of an operational military decision?

If so, consider the Fourth Circuit's decision in *Al Shimari v. CACI Premier Technology, Inc.*, 840 F.3d 147 (4th Cir. 2016). There, the Court of Appeals held that claims arising out of a private military contractor's alleged abuses of U.S. military detainees while operating a prison in Iraq did not necessarily present a political question. The distinction on which *Al Shimari* turned was whether the plaintiffs' claims were that the defendants acted *unlawfully*, and not just tortiously. *See id.* at 158.

In *bin Ali Jaber*, the D.C. Circuit criticized *Al Shimari*, observing that such reasoning "puts the cart before the horse, requiring the district court to first decide the merits of a claim and, only thereafter, determine whether that claim was justiciable." 2017 WL 2818645, at *4 n.1. The D.C. Circuit's observation is clearly incorrect; the question the Fourth Circuit posed was whether the plaintiffs *alleged* that the defendants acted unlawfully, not whether they could in fact *prove* their allegations. But what do you think of the larger premise, *i.e.*, that there is, and should be, a meaningful distinction for purposes of the political question doctrine between claims that the military or its agents acted unlawfully (which *Al Shimari* holds that courts can and should resolve) and claims that the military or its agents acted lawfully but unreasonably (which *Al Shimari* agrees present non-justiciable political questions)?

[NSL p. 158. Replace Subsection C.1. A Cause of Action?]

1. A Cause of Action?

Congress has enacted a small number of statutes that create causes of action or create jurisdiction in federal courts for claims that may have some bearing on national security. Examples include the Antiterrorism Act, 18 U.S.C. §2333 (2012 & Supp. IV 2016) (creating a civil damages claim for U.S. nationals injured by reason of an act of international terrorism), the Torture Victim Protection Act, Pub. L. No. 102-256, 106 Stat. 73 (1992) (codified at 28 U.S.C. §1350 note (2012)) (providing a civil remedy for victims of torture or extrajudicial killing), and the Foreign Intelligence Surveillance Act (FISA), 50 U.S.C. §1810 (2012) (creating a cause of action for individuals who are "aggrieved" by certain unlawful searches under FISA). It has also provided federal jurisdiction for at least some customary international law claims against aliens. Alien Tort Statute, 28 U.S.C. §1350 (2012); *see Sosa v. Alvarez-Machain*, 542 U.S. 692 (2004).

Congress has also provided for suits against the federal government that may implicate national security. For example, the Administrative Procedure Act (APA) provides that "[a] person suffering legal wrong because of agency action, or adversely affected or aggrieved by agency action within the meaning of a relevant statute, is entitled to judicial review thereof." 5 U.S.C. §702 (2012). APA review, however, is generally limited to "final" agency actions, and it does not apply to military commissions or "military authority exercised in the field in time of war or in occupied territory." 5 U.S.C. §701(b)(1)(G) (2012).

In addition, the Tucker Act, 28 U.S.C. §1491 (2012), waives sovereign immunity for contract and other non-tort claims against the federal government. And the Federal Tort Claims Act, 28 U.S.C. §§1346(b), 2671-2680 (2012 & Supp. I 2013), does the same for actions against the United States "for injury or loss of property, or personal injury or death caused by the negligent or wrongful act or omission of any employee of the Government while acting within the scope of his office or employment," *id.* §1346(b)(1), but not if the tort arose from the exercise of "discretionary functions," *id.* §2680(a), or "combatant activities." *Id.* §2680(j). Nor is recovery permitted for "[a]ny claim arising in a foreign country" or for "intentional torts" committed by non-law enforcement officers. *Id.* §2680(k). And the Supreme Court has ruled that claims are barred for "injuries to servicemen where the injuries arise out of or are in the course of activity incident to service." *Feres v. United States*, 340 U.S. 135, 146 (1950).

In addition to these statutory remedies, plaintiffs who seek relief for an injury caused by federal government action in violation of a constitutional right may attempt to assert an implied right of action. Although the existence of such a cause of action for injunctive relief against ongoing government action is well-established, the ability to obtain damages for constitutional violations that have ceased is much murkier. In *Bivens v. Six Unknown Named Agents of Fed. Bureau of Narcotics*, 403 U.S. 388 (1971), the Supreme Court recognized a cause of action for damages against federal narcotics agents who allegedly violated the plaintiff's Fourth Amendment rights by an illegal search. The Court declared:

> Of course, the Fourth Amendment does not in so many words provide for its enforcement by an award of money damages for the consequences of its violation. But "it is . . . well settled that where legal rights have been invaded, and a federal statute provides for a general right to sue for such invasion, federal courts may use any available remedy to make good the wrong done." *Bell v. Hood*, 327 U.S. [678,] 684 [(1946)] (footnote omitted.) The present case involves no special factors counseling hesitation in the absence of affirmative action by Congress. [*Id.* at 396.]

Subsequently, courts have inferred private rights of action under the First, Fifth, and Eighth Amendments, as well. *See* Erwin Chemerinsky, *Federal Jurisdiction* 611 (5th ed. 2007). However, the Supreme Court in recent years has repeatedly relied upon the caveats identified in *Bivens* — where Congress has provided an alternative remedy or where there are special factors counseling hesitation — to decline to recognize new

Bivens remedies. *See id.* at 615. One of the "special factors" the Justices have identified is presented when a military service member seeks a remedy for "injuries that arise out of or are in the course of activity incident to military service." *United States v. Stanley*, 483 U.S. 669, 684 (1987) (quoting *Feres, supra*).

And in *Ziglar* v. *Abbasi*, 137 S. Ct. 1843 (2017), a case arising out of the post-September 11 immigration "roundup" of young men of Muslim and/or Arab descent in and around New York City (discussed at length in casebook Chapter 31, pp. 961-979), a 4-2 majority of the Supreme Court expressed serious skepticism that *Bivens* claims will *ever* be appropriate in national security cases. As Justice Kennedy explained,

> National-security policy is the prerogative of the Congress and President. *See* U.S. Const. Art. I, §8; Art. II, §1, §2. Judicial inquiry into the national-security realm raises "concerns for the separation of powers in trenching on matters committed to the other branches." *Christopher v. Harbury*, 536 U.S. 403, 417 (2002). *These concerns are even more pronounced when the judicial inquiry comes in the context of a claim seeking money damages rather than a claim seeking injunctive or other equitable relief.* The risk of personal damages liability is more likely to cause an official to second-guess difficult but necessary decisions concerning national-security policy. [*Id.* at 1849 (emphasis added).]

The *Ziglar* Court went out of its way to reaffirm the viability of claims that present facts similar to those in *Bivens*. *See id.* at 1856 ("[T]his opinion is not intended to cast doubt on the continued force, or even the necessity, of *Bivens* in the search-and-seizure context in which it arose."). But the Court then emphasized that the relevant question to ask in *Bivens* cases is whether "the case is different in a meaningful way from previous *Bivens* cases decided by *this* Court." *Id.* at 1859 (emphasis added). Given that the Supreme Court has only expressly affirmed *Bivens* claims in three circumstances, this statement is likely to cabin the expansion of *Bivens* — especially in contexts, such as challenges to national security or counterterrorism policies (or the enforcement thereof), in which it has not previously thrived.

Whatever one thinks of judge-made remedies in general, does the distinction at the core of *Ziglar* — between prospective relief (such as injunctions) and retrospective relief (such as damages) — strike you as normatively satisfying? If the separation-of-powers concern animating the Court's hostility to judge-made damages suits is, as Justice Kennedy suggests, that courts might "interfere in an intrusive way with sensitive functions of the Executive Branch," *id.* at 1861, why is that not a much larger concern in suits seeking to enjoin an ongoing government action, like military operations, than in suits seeking retrospective relief in the form of damages years (or, as in *Ziglar*, more than a decade) after the fact? Indeed, is there any argument that we should *prefer* damages over injunctions in national security cases, given the difficulty, both factually and legally, of fully ascertaining the validity of government action as it is ongoing? This was the argument with which Justice Breyer closed his dissent:

> [T]here may well be a particular need for *Bivens* remedies when security-related Government actions are at issue. History tells us of far too many instances where the Executive or Legislative Branch took actions during time of war that, on later examination, turned out unnecessarily and unreasonably to have deprived American citizens of basic constitutional rights. . . .
>
> . . . Complaints seeking [prospective] relief typically come during the emergency itself, when emotions are strong, when courts may have too little or inaccurate information, and when courts may well prove particularly reluctant to interfere with even the least well-founded Executive Branch activity. . . .
>
> A damages action, however, is typically brought after the emergency is over, after emotions have cooled, and at a time when more factual information is available. In such circumstances, courts have more time to exercise such judicial virtues as calm reflection and dispassionate application of the law to the facts. . . . I should think that the wisdom of permitting courts to consider *Bivens* actions, later granting monetary compensation to those wronged at the time, would follow *a fortiori*. [*Id.* at 1884 (Breyer, J., dissenting).]

If it comes down to a choice between prospective and retrospective relief in national security cases, which of these approaches do you find more convincing? Why?

Regardless of who has the better of this argument, note the most important consequence of *Ziglar*: the absence of a cause of action for damages is fatal to a claim for any retrospective judicial relief whatever, regardless of the *merits* of such a claim — even for the most egregious and clearly established constitutional violations. In the context of the political question doctrine cases discussed above, why won't such a holding confer a form of "absolute" immunity, such that federal government officers never have to fear damages liability for constitutional violations in national security litigation (if not more generally)? If Congress disagrees with this result, how might it avoid it?

[NSL p. 182. Insert at the end of Note 6.]

The U.S. withdrawal from the Paris Agreement on climate change and speculation about U.S. abrogation of the Iran Nuclear Agreement have raised related questions about executive power to change or terminate international agreements. *See* Stephen P. Mulligan, *Withdrawal from International Agreements: Legal Framework, the Paris Agreement, and the Iran Nuclear Agreement* (Cong. Res. Serv. R44761), Feb. 9, 2017.

[NSL p. 239, CTL p. 49. Insert before Note 1.]

   0. *Vacated and remanded.* The Supreme Court granted certiorari in *Hernandez*, and then vacated and remanded in a per curiam opinion. *Hernandez v. Mesa*, 137 S. Ct. 2003 (2017) (per curiam). But the opinion for the Court dodged the question of the extraterritorial application of the Fourth and Fifth Amendments, instead remanding for the lower court to consider whether Hernandez had a *Bivens* remedy for damages under the Fifth Amendment (see NSL p. 158-160), in light of its decision in *Ziglar v. Abbasi*, 137 S. Ct. 1843 (2017), denying a *Bivens* remedy to detainees rounded up after 9/11. *See* this *Supplement* pp. 8. Justice Breyer, joined by Justice Ginsburg, dissented, making six arguments (complete with a map and pictures) to the effect that the culvert in which the Hernandez's son was shot *is* the border for constitutional purposes, or at least a special border-related area (called a "limitrophe") that raises unique questions of extraterritorial application. *See* 137 S. Ct. at 2008-2010 (Breyer, J., dissenting).
   The Court also held that the lower court improperly granted qualified immunity to the defendant Border Patrol officer in reliance on the fact that the decedent had no significant relationship to the United States. But qualified immunity depends on facts known to the defendant officer at the time of the conduct, not what they learn afterwards. *See id.* at 2007 (majority opinion). The Court therefore remanded for the court of appeals to revisit the immunity defense, although it strongly suggested that the case could be resolved, in light of *Abbasi*, solely on the *Bivens* questions. *See id.* at 2006-2007.

[NSL p. 239, CTL p. 49. Insert at the end of Note 3.]

See generally Mark Binelli, *The Killing of a Mexican 16-year-old Raises Troubling Questions about the United States Border Patrol*, N.Y. Times (Mag.) 36 (Mar. 6, 2016) (describing shooting of José Rodriquez and reporting that the defendant Border Patrol officer in the civil lawsuit has been indicted for second-degree murder for shooting Rodriguez — the first Border Patrol officer to be prosecuted for a cross-border shooting).

———————

[NSL p. 249, CTL p. 59. Insert at end of Note 4.]

In *Jesner v. Arab Bank*, the Acting Solicitor General urged the Supreme Court to remand for the court of appeals to consider whether the dollar-clearing activities in the United States of a Jordanian bank charged with funding terrorism in Israel sufficiently "touches and concerns" the United States to support application of the ATS to the bank's activities. Brief for the United States as *Amicus Curiae* Supporting Neither Party at 25-30, *Jesner v. Arab Bank, PLC*, 137 S. Ct. 1432 (2017) (No. 16-499) (mem.). Should it make a difference whether the bank conducted dollar-clearing through third-party correspondent banks or through its own U.S. branch?

———————

[NSL p. 313, CTL p. 137. Insert at the end of Note 7.]

Twice in 2016 the Obama administration revised the *Department of Defense Law of War Manual, supra,* to better protect civilians in combat. July 2016 revisions were focused on protecting journalists working in battlefield areas. December 2016 changes tightened rules for when it is lawful to fire on a military target where civilians, including human shields and civilian workers at weapons factories, are nearby. The changes are reflected largely in the discussion of the principle of proportionality. While the original version of the *Manual* suggested that commanders could exclude entire categories of civilians when analyzing proportionality before targeting — including human shields, civilians accompanying an enemy force, and civilians working at munitions factories — the revisions make clear that commanders must take these groups into account in assessing the anticipated harm to civilians. Charlie Savage, *To Protect Civilians, Pentagon Tightens Rules on Combat*, N.Y. Times, Dec. 14, 2006. Do you agree that these changes to the *Manual* were warranted? Can you think of other precautions that should be explicitly factored into a proportionality analysis?

[NSL p. 323. Add to second full paragraph.]

In 2016, it was reported that on October 22, 1968, presidential candidate Richard M. Nixon, in anticipation of the election two weeks later, directed his top aide, H.R. Haldeman, to "monkey wrench" efforts to bring the war to a quick end. *See* John A. Farrell, Op-ed., *Nixon's Vietnam Treachery*, N.Y. Times, Dec. 31, 2016.

[NSL p. 361. Insert after Note 2.]

E. A RECENT TEST OF THE COURTS' ROLE

Smith v. Obama
United States District Court, District of Columbia, Nov. 21, 2016
217 F. Supp. 3d 283

COLLEEN KOLLAR-KOTELLY, United States District Judge. Plaintiff is a U.S. Army Captain who was deployed, until recently, to the Kuwait headquarters of the Combined Joint Task Force-Operation Inherent Resolve. Operation Inherent Resolve is the designation the U.S. Department of Defense has given to the military campaign against the Islamic State of Iraq and the Levant ("ISIL") initiated by the United States and its allies in 2014. Plaintiff considers the operation to be a "good war" and "what [he] signed up to be part of when [he] joined the military." Nonetheless, Plaintiff seeks a declaration that Operation Inherent Resolve is illegal because Congress has not authorized it. Specifically, Plaintiff alleges that President Barack H. Obama has not sought Congress' authorization for military action against ISIL in accordance with the War Powers Resolution, and that neither the President's Commander-in-Chief power, nor prior Congressional authorizations for the use of force, give the President the authority to continue these actions. Plaintiff acknowledges that whether military action has been duly authorized is generally a question "Congress is supposed to answer," but complains that Congress is "AWOL." Plaintiff also claims that the Take Care Clause requires President Obama to publish a "sustained legal justification" for Operation Inherent Resolve to enable Plaintiff to determine for himself whether this military action is consistent with his oath to preserve and protect the Constitution.

Before the Court is Defendant's Motion to Dismiss. Defendant argues that this Court lacks jurisdiction over Plaintiff's claims for a number of reasons. Specifically, Defendant argues that (1) Plaintiff's claims raise non-justiciable political questions, (2) Plaintiff lacks standing. . . .

I. BACKGROUND

A. Operation Inherent Resolve

On September 10, 2014, President Obama announced to the American people that America would "lead a broad coalition to roll back" the "terrorist threat" posed by ISIL.[3] The President announced that the United States would "degrade and ultimately destroy ISIL through a comprehensive and sustained counterterrorism strategy," which included "a systematic campaign of airstrikes," increased "support to forces fighting these terrorists on the ground," counterterrorism strategies, and humanitarian assistance. *Id.* The President stated that he had "secured bipartisan support for this approach here at home," and that although he had "the authority to address the threat from ISIL," he "welcome[d] congressional support for this effort in order to show the world that Americans are united in confronting this danger." *Id.* The Department of Defense later designated this effort "Operation Inherent Resolve."

Following his address, on September 23, 2014, the President sent a letter to Congress reiterating that he had "ordered implementation of a new comprehensive and sustained counterterrorism strategy to degrade, and ultimately defeat, ISIL."[5] In this letter, President Obama explained the military actions he had ordered, and stated that:

---

3. President Barack H. Obama, *Statement by the President on ISIL* (Sept. 10, 2014), https://www.gpo.gov/fdsys/pkg/DCPD-201400654/pdf/DCPD-201400654.pdf.

5. President Barack H. Obama, *Letter to Congressional Leaders Reporting on the Deployment of United States Armed Forces Personnel To Iraq and the Authorization of Military Operations in Syria* (Sept. 23, 2014), https://www.gpo.gov/fdsys/pkg/DCPD-201400697/pdf/DCPD201400697.pdf.

I have directed these actions, which are in the national security and foreign policy interests of the United States, pursuant to my constitutional and statutory authority as Commander in Chief (including the authority to carry out Public Law 107-40 and Public Law 107-243) and as Chief Executive, as well as my constitutional and statutory authority to conduct the foreign relations of the United States.

I am providing this report as part of my efforts to keep the Congress fully informed, consistent with the War Powers Resolution (Public Law 93-148). I appreciate the support of the Congress in this action.

Id. Public Law 107-40 and Public Law 107-243, referenced by the President, were passed by Congress in 2001 and 2002, and each constitute[s] specific authorization for the use of military force. First, in response to the terrorist attacks of September 11, 2001, Congress passed a Joint Resolution to "authorize the use of United States Armed Forces against those responsible for the recent attacks launched against the United States." Authorization for Use of Military Force, Pub. L. No. 107-40, 115 Stat. 224 (2001) ("2001 AUMF") [casebook p. 375]. The 2001 AUMF states that "the President is authorized to use all necessary and appropriate force against those nations, organizations, or persons he determines planned, authorized, committed, or aided the terrorist attacks that occurred on September 11, 2001, or harbored such organizations or persons, in order to prevent any future acts of international terrorism against the United States by such nations, organizations or persons." Pub. L. No. 107-40, §2(a). It also states that "[c]onsistent with section 8(a)(1) of the War Powers Resolution, the Congress declares that this section is intended to constitute specific statutory authorization within the meaning of section 5(b) of the War Powers Resolution." Pub. L. No. 107-40, §2(b)(1).

Second, in 2002 Congress passed a Joint Resolution authorizing the President "to use the Armed Forces of the United States as he determines to be necessary and appropriate in order to . . . defend the national security of the United States against the continuing threat posed by Iraq." Authorization for Use of Military Force against Iraq Resolution of 2002, Pub. L. No. 107-243, §3(a)(1), 116 Stat. 1498 (2002) ("2002 AUMF") [casebook p. 372]. The 2002 AUMF also states that "[c]onsistent with section 8(a)(1) of the War Powers Resolution, the Congress declares that this section is intended to constitute specific statutory authorization within the meaning of section 5(b) of the War Powers Resolution." Pub. L. No. 107-243, §3(c)(1).

. . . [I]n a speech . . . at an annual meeting of the American Society of International Law on April 10, 2015 . . . [Stephen W. Preston, the

General Counsel of the Department of Defense] explained that ISIL was an appropriate target under the 2001 AUMF because the group had long fought the United States alongside al Qaeda, which was responsible for the September 11th attacks. Preston stated that ISIL had previously been known as al Qaeda in Iraq after its leader, Abu Musab al-Zarqawi, had pledged his allegiance to Osama bin Laden in 2004. *Id.* . . . . He went on to explain that:

> The recent split between ISIL and current al-Qa'ida leadership does not remove ISIL from coverage under the 2001 AUMF, because ISIL continues to wage the conflict against the United States that it entered into when, in 2004, it joined bin Laden's al-Qa'ida organization in its conflict against the United States. . . . ISIL continues to denounce the United States as its enemy and to target U.S. citizens and interests. . . .

Id. Preston also explained that "[t]he President's authority to fight ISIL is further reinforced by the" 2002 AUMF because "[a]lthough the threat posed by Saddam Hussein's regime in Iraq was the primary focus of the 2002 AUMF, the statute, in accordance with its express goals, has always been understood to authorize the use of force for the related purposes of helping to establish a stable, democratic Iraq and addressing terrorist threats emanating from Iraq." *Id.* . . .

III. DISCUSSION . . .

A. Standing

. . . On the specific facts of this case, and in particular due to the narrow and unique legal injury that Plaintiff asserts, the Court finds that Plaintiff lacks standing.

"Standing to sue is a doctrine rooted in the traditional understanding of a case or controversy." *Spokeo, Inc. v. Robins*, ___ U.S. ___, 136 S. Ct. 1540, 1547 (2016), *as revised* (May 24, 2016). To establish standing, Plaintiff bears the burden of demonstrating that he "(1) suffered an injury in fact, (2) that is fairly traceable to the challenged conduct of the defendant, and (3) that is likely to be redressed by a favorable judicial decision." *Id.* (citing *Lujan v. Defs. of Wildlife*, 504 U.S. 555, 560-61 (1992)). . . . The Court notes that the standing inquiry is "especially rigorous when reaching the merits of the dispute would force [the Court] to decide whether an action taken by one of the other two branches of the Federal Government was unconstitutional." *Raines v. Byrd*, 521 U.S.

811, 819-20 (1997). . . .

As a starting point, Plaintiff's bare disagreement with, or simple uncertainty about the legality of, President Obama's decision to take military action against ISIL does not constitute an injury in fact. Such disagreement or uncertainty presents no "concrete" harm, nor is it "particularized" because it does not affect Plaintiff in any individual or particular way. It is well-established that "a bare assertion that the government is engaging in illegal or unconstitutional activity does not allege injury sufficient to confer standing." *Haitian Refugee Ctr. v. Gracey*, 809 F.2d 794, 799 (D.C. Cir. 1987). In other words, "the psychological consequence presumably produced by observation of conduct with which one disagrees," is not an injury in fact. *Valley Forge Christian Coll. v. Ams. United for Separation of Church & State, Inc.*, 454 U.S. 464, 485 (1982). From this baseline, it is Plaintiff's burden to clearly allege some additional concrete, particularized harm that the alleged violations caused or threaten to cause him.

. . . Plaintiff does not allege the traditional types of injuries one might expect a service person challenging the legality of military action to allege. Plaintiff *does not* allege that he suffers any injury in the form of physical or emotional harms, or the risk thereof, associated with deployment to a theatre of combat. He also *does not* allege that he has been involuntarily forced to participate in a military action in violation of his own constitutional rights or liberties. And he *does not* allege that he has any moral or philosophical objections to the military action against ISIL. Indeed, Plaintiff has no qualms about participating in a fight against ISIL, and his lawsuit does not seek to relieve him of his obligation to do so. . . .

Instead, the Court discerns two different types of harms for which Plaintiff seeks relief. First, Plaintiff alleges that he "suffers legal injury because, to provide support for an illegal war, he must violate his oath to 'preserve, protect, and defend the Constitution of the United States.'" In addition, Plaintiff alleges that he is at risk of being punished for disobeying legally-given orders. . . .

1. *Little v. Barreme* Does Not Require Plaintiff to Disobey Orders

First, Plaintiff seeks to base his standing on the Supreme Court case *Little v. Barreme*, 6 U.S. (2 Cranch) 170 (1804) [casebook p. 90]. Plaintiff argues that this case stands for the proposition that "military officers must disobey orders that are beyond the legal authorization of their commander-in-chief." Plaintiff reads too much into *Little*.

Little concerned a 1799 non-intercourse law whereby Congress had authorized President John Adams to order his naval commanders to seize American merchant ships sailing *to* French ports, but had not authorized the seizure of ships sailing *from* French ports. *Little*, 6 U.S. at 170. On orders from the Secretary of the Navy, one naval commander acted beyond the scope of this authorization and seized a ship sailing *from* a French port. *Id.* at 171-72. The owner of the seized vessel sued the commander. *Id.* at 172. Chief Justice John Marshall held that the commander was liable in damages to the owner of the vessel, and that the President's instructions to the commander were not a defense to that liability. *Id.* at 179. Justice Marshall explained that "the instructions cannot change the nature of the transaction, or legalize an act which without those instructions would have been a plain trespass." *Id.*

As the Supreme Court has since explained, *Little* stands for the proposition that "a federal official [is] protected for action tortious under state law only if his acts were authorized by controlling federal law." *Butz v. Economou*, 438 U.S. 478, 490 (1978). *Little* does not stand for the proposition, as Plaintiff argues, that military personnel have a *duty to disobey* orders they believe are beyond Congressional authorization. There is a significant difference between a holding that Presidential authorization for an act beyond Congressional authority does not *immunize* military personnel from tort liability under state law, and a holding that military personnel *must disobey* orders that they believe are beyond such authority. Plaintiff points the Court to no authority that has interpreted *Little* to stand for the latter proposition, and the Court has found none.

To the contrary, it appears well-settled in the post-*Little* era that there is no right, let alone a duty, to disobey military orders simply because one questions the Congressional authorization of the broader military effort. *See U.S. ex rel. New v. Rumsfeld*, 448 F.3d 403, 411 (D.C. Cir. 2006) (in the context of challenging a military order that plaintiff alleged was given in violation of the United Nations Participation Act, holding that "nothing gives a soldier 'authority for a self-help remedy of disobedience'") (quoting *United States v. New*, 55 M.J. 95, 108 (C.A.A.F. 2001)); *United States v. Huet-Vaughn*, 43 M.J. 105, 114 (C.A.A.F. 1995) (" . . . The so-called 'Nuremberg defense' applies only to individual acts committed in wartime; it does not apply to the Government's decision to wage war."); *see also New*, 55 M.J. at 109 ("The duty to disobey an unlawful order applies only to a positive act that constitutes a crime that is so manifestly beyond the legal power or discretion of the commander as to admit of no rational doubt of their unlawfulness.") (quoting *Huet-Vaughn*, 43 M.J. at 114).

Nor does the oath Plaintiff was required to swear as an officer in the Army change this outcome. The modern oath for officers requires the officer to swear to "support and defend the Constitution." 5 U.S.C. §3331. Plaintiff argues that this oath reinforces his interpretation of *Little* and further requires him to disobey orders he believes may exceed congressional authorization. Again, the Court disagrees. An oath to "support" the Constitution does not "involve[ ] nebulous, undefined responsibilities for action in some hypothetical situations," but has instead "been interpreted to mean simply a commitment to abide by our constitutional system." *Cole v. Richardson*, 405 U.S. 676, 684 (1972). Although, as discussed below, such an oath may require Plaintiff to refrain from violating the Constitution, *see infra* §III.A.2, Plaintiff offers no real support for the extremely expansive and apparently novel interpretation of the officer's oath that would require disobedience of military orders based on an officer's legal interpretation of whether Congress had properly authorized the broader military effort. Beyond the fact that there is no legal support for such a proposition, the Court finds persuasive Defendant's argument regarding the obvious and problematic practical consequences such an interpretation would have on military effectiveness. Namely, that it would leave "individual service members to decide which orders to follow based on their individual assessment of" whether the order falls within prior Congressional authorizations for the use of military force.

Because neither *Little* nor Plaintiff's oath can plausibly be read to *require* Plaintiff to disobey his orders, Plaintiff was not forced to experience or risk concrete and particularized harms associated with wrongful disobedience, such as court-martial or dishonorable discharge. In other words, Plaintiff had "an 'available course of action which subject[ed] [him] to no concrete adverse consequences' — he [could] obey the orders of the Commander-in-Chief." *Drake v. Obama*, 664 F.3d 774, 780 (9th Cir. 2011). Doing so would have neither subjected Plaintiff to discipline, nor been unlawful. *See* Dep't of Def., Law of War Manual, §18.3.2.1 (May 2016) ("[S]ubordinates are not required to screen the orders of superiors for questionable points of legality, and may, absent specific knowledge to the contrary, presume that orders have been lawfully issued."). The risk of military punishment for disobedience, therefore, does not give Plaintiff standing.

2. Plaintiff Does Not Have Standing Under the "Oath of Office" Cases

Plaintiff also seeks to base his standing on "oath of office" cases [chiefly *Board of Education of Central School District No. 1 v. Allen*, 392 U.S. 236 (1968)]. These cases generally stand for the proposition that an official who has taken an oath to support the Constitution has standing to challenge a government action if he or she is then forced to choose between violating the Constitution and facing concrete harm. . . .

. . . Plaintiff in this case alleges that President Obama has violated a statute, the War Powers Resolution, by not seeking Congressional authorization for military actions against ISIL, and violated the Take Care Clause of the Constitution by failing to publish an explanation of the legal justifications for these actions. Even accepting these allegations as true, Plaintiff fails to allege that *he* . . . is being asked to undertake any action that would be a violation of the Constitution and therefore his oath. . . .

. . . The Court acknowledges that Plaintiff questions the legality of, or congressional authorization for, an enterprise he was involved with — Operation Inherent Resolve. However, even assuming that Plaintiff is correct that the President violated the War Powers Resolution, it does not follow that any act Plaintiff himself was asked to take as an intelligence officer in that Operation would itself be unconstitutional. . . . [T]he alleged violation of the War Powers Resolution in this case is based solely on the alleged actions, or lack thereof, of President Obama, not Plaintiff. The same is true with regard to the alleged violation of the Take Care Clause. Plaintiff violates neither by participating in Operation Inherent Resolve. . . . Plaintiff here is at least one step removed from these allegations of illegality or unconstitutionality. Even accepting his allegations as true, he is not himself being ordered to violate the Constitution, and therefore his oath. . . .

3. Plaintiff Does Not Allege Physical or Individual Liberty-Based Injuries

Finally, the Court rejects Plaintiff's argument that the "decisions in cases brought by service members challenging the Vietnam War further confirm [Plaintiff's] standing." To be sure, such cases do stand for the proposition that service men and women ordered into a war that they contend is illegal may have standing to challenge that war, and the Court finds the reasoning of those cases logical and persuasive. *See Berk v.*

Laird, 429 F.2d 302 (2d Cir. 1970); *Massachusetts v. Laird*, 451 F.2d 26 (1st Cir. 1971) [both cases noted at p. 335]. The Court does not question as a general matter the apparent assumption of certain courts that service members may be appropriate parties to challenge the legality of military action that they claim endangers them.

These cases do not, however, address the novel legal injury put forth by Plaintiff. In the cases referred to by Plaintiff, plaintiff-service members claimed that they were being forced to fight in violation of their constitutional rights, and the injuries that they alleged were the deprivation of liberty and the risk of injury or death. *See Berk*, 429 F.2d at 304 (soldier ordered to dispatch to Vietnam alleging violations of his constitutional rights could bring suit challenging legality of war where "the complaint can be construed as putting in controversy his future earning capacity, which serious injury or even death might diminish by an amount exceeding $10,000"); *Massachusetts v. Laird*, 451 F.2d at 28 (soldiers serving in Southeast Asia had standing to challenge Vietnam War where "[t]hey allege[d] that their forced service in an undeclared war is a deprivation of liberty in violation of the due process clause of the Fifth Amendment").

Plaintiff in this case has made it abundantly clear that these are not the legal injuries for which he is seeking redress. Although Plaintiff claims that "[t]he injuries that threaten [Plaintiff] are *also* concrete," (emphasis added), he does not seek to base his standing on the fact that he risks bodily or individual liberty-based injuries as alleged by past service member plaintiffs. In fact, the relief sought by Plaintiff would not prevent the risk of these injuries. To the contrary, Plaintiff defines the relief he seeks as being able to "continue fighting," but simply "without confronting the dilemma imposed upon [him] by *Little* and [his] oath of office." . . . These cases are accordingly inapposite and do not support Plaintiff's claim that the "dilemma" he faces constitutes an injury-in-fact. . . .

In sum, the Court concludes that the "injuries" upon which Plaintiff grounds his claim do not constitute "injury in fact" as required to support Article III standing. Plaintiff argues that his oath of office, in combination with the Supreme Court's ruling in *Little*, place him in an untenable "dilemma" that can only be resolved by this Court's deciding the lawfulness of the President's actions. The Court disagrees. Neither *Little* nor Plaintiff's oath require[s] him to disobey his orders. Nor is Plaintiff forced to choose between violating the Constitution or suffering concrete harm, like plaintiffs in past cases where "oath of office" standing has been accepted. The Court draws no conclusions as to the standing of a service member ordered into a war he or she believes is unlawful where the soldier's claim is based on his own constitutional rights, individual liberties, physical or emotional well-being, or other injuries. This case simply does not present those questions.

B. The Political Question Doctrine

The Court also finds that dismissal is appropriate under the political question doctrine. . . .

. . . Plaintiff's claims are premised on the notion that Congress has not previously authorized the use of force against ISIL. Defendant disputes this. Resolving this dispute would require the Court to determine whether the legal authorizations for the use of military force relied on by President Obama — the 2001 and 2002 AUMFs — in fact authorize the use of force against ISIL. With regard to the 2001 AUMF, the Court would have to determine whether the President is correct that ISIL is among "those nations, organizations, or persons" that "planned, authorized, committed, or aided the terrorist attacks that occurred on September 11, 2001, or harbored such organizations or persons," and that Operation Inherent Resolve represents "necessary and appropriate force" against that group. Pub. L. No. 107-40, §2(a). With regard to the 2002 AUMF, the Court would have to determine whether the President is correct that operations against ISIL are "necessary and appropriate in order to . . . defend the national security of the United States against the continuing threat posed by Iraq." Pub. L. No. 107-243, §3(a)(1). For the reasons set out below, the Court finds that these are political questions under the first two *Baker* [v. *Carr*, 369 U.S. 186 (1962)] factors: the issues raised are primarily ones committed to the political branches of government, and the Court lacks judicially manageable standards, and is otherwise ill-equipped, to resolve them.

There can be "no doubt that decision-making in the fields of foreign policy and national security is textually committed to the political branches of government." *Schneider* [v. *Kissinger*, 412 F.3d 190 (2005)] at 194; *see also Gilligan* [v. *Morgan*, 413 U.S. 1 (1973) at 10 ("It would be difficult to think of a clearer example of the type of governmental action that was intended by the Constitution to be left to the political branches . . . [than the] complex, subtle, and professional decisions as to the . . . control of a military force . . . ."); *Luftig v. McNamara*, 373 F.2d 664, 665-66 (D.C. Cir. 1967) ("The fundamental division of authority and power established by the Constitution precludes judges from overseeing the conduct of foreign policy or the use and disposition of military power; these matters are plainly the exclusive province of Congress and the Executive.").

Questions of statutory construction and interpretation, however, are committed to the Judiciary, and Plaintiff argues that this is a "garden-variety statutory construction case," that presents "straightforward problems of statutory interpretation." The principle that resolving questions of statutory interpretation, and the constitutionality of statutes, is a task committed to the Judiciary was recently reiterated by the Supreme Court in *Zivotofsky ex rel. Zivotofsky v. Clinton,* 132 S. Ct. 1421 (2012) [casebook p. 71]. . . .

. . . Although, as in *Zivotofsky,* statutes are *involved* in this case — in particular, the War Powers Resolution, the 2001 AUMF and the 2002 AUMF — this case does not present nearly the same fundamental legal issues as were at issue in *Zivotofsky.* The questions posed in this case go significantly beyond interpreting statutes and determining whether they are constitutional. Plaintiff asks the Court to second-guess the Executive's *application* of these statutes to specific facts on the ground in an ongoing combat mission halfway around the world. For example, the Court is not asked simply to "interpret" the 2001 AUMF, or to determine its constitutionality. It is asked to determine whether the President is correct that ISIL, as it exists today, is an appropriate target under that resolution based on the nature and extent of ISIL's relationship and connections with the terrorist organization that the President has determined was responsible for the September 11, 2001 attacks. The Court would also have to go further than simply "interpreting" the 2002 AUMF. It would have to determine whether the President is correct that the ongoing military action against ISIL is in fact "necessary and appropriate in order to . . . defend the national security of the United States against the continuing threat posed by Iraq." Pub. L. No. 107-243, §3(a)(1).

The reality, then, is more nuanced than Plaintiff suggests. Plaintiff's claims raise mixed questions of both discretionary military judgment *and* statutory interpretation. The Court does not read *Zivotofsky* as foreclosing the application of the political question doctrine under this scenario. Rather, under the particular facts of this case, the Court determines that dismissal under that doctrine is in fact warranted for three reasons.

First, certain aspects of the questions posed by this case are indisputably and completely committed to the political branches of government. Both the 2001 and 2002 AUMFs authorize only that force that the President determines is "necessary and appropriate." Pub. L. No.

107-40, §2(a); Pub. L. No. 107-243, §3(a)(1). The necessity and appropriateness of military action is precisely the type of discretionary military determination that is committed to the political branches and which the Court has no judicially manageable standards to adjudicate.

Second, whatever factual questions are raised by Plaintiff's claims are not of the type that the Court is well-equipped to resolve. Instead, the particular questions presented in this case "require judicial inquiry into sensitive military matters" about which "[t]he Court lacks the resources and expertise (which are accessible to the Congress) to resolve disputed questions of fact concerning." *Crockett v. Reagan*, 558 F. Supp. 893, 898 (D.D.C. 1982), *aff'd*, 720 F.2d 1355 (D.C. Cir. 1983) (dismissing claim that the President violated the War Powers Resolution under the political question doctrine, holding that "[t]he subtleties of factfinding in this situation should be left to the political branches."); *Crockett v. Reagan*, 720 F.2d 1355, 1356 (D.C. Cir. 1983) (affirming the trial court's reasoning in dismissing the case because it "did not have the resources or expertise to resolve the particular factual disputes involved in this case").

Based on the pleadings thus far alone, the Court can easily discern that this case raises factual questions that are not of a type the Court is equipped to handle with traditional judicially manageable standards. The President and Department of Defense officials apparently believe that ISIL is connected with al Qaeda and that, despite public rifts, some allegiances between the groups persist and ISIL continues to pursue the same mission today as it did before allegedly splintering from al Qaeda. Plaintiff disputes these factual assertions, relying on an affidavit from scholars of Islamic Law that argue that as of today, the groups are in fact sufficiently distinct, and potentially even antagonistic, that they can no longer be viewed as the same terrorist organization. Resolving this dispute would require inquiries into sensitive military determinations, presumably made based on intelligence collected on the ground in a live theatre of combat, and potentially changing and developing on an ongoing basis. *See Al-Aulaqi v. Obama*, 727 F. Supp. 2d 1, 45 (D.D.C. 2010) ("The difficulty that U.S. courts would encounter if they were tasked with 'ascertaining the 'facts' of military decisions exercised thousands of miles from the forum, lies at the heart of the determination whether the question [posed] is a 'political' one.'") (quoting *DaCosta v. Laird*, 471 F.2d 1146, 1148 (2d Cir. 1973)).

Finally, an additional factor makes judicial intervention particularly inappropriate on the specific facts of this case. Unlike the situation presented in *Zivotofsky*, the Court in this case is not presented with a dispute between the two political branches regarding the challenged

action. In fact, Congress has repeatedly provided funding for the effort
against ISIL. For example, on November 10, 2014, President Obama sent
a letter to the Speaker of the House of Representatives requesting that
Congress consider proposed amendments to the 2015 Budget to provide
funding for Operation Inherent Resolve. The letter explained that
"[t]hese amendments would provide $5.6 billion for OCO activities to
degrade and ultimately defeat the Islamic State of Iraq and the Levant
(ISIL) — including military operations as part of Operation Inherent
Resolve."[12] President Obama also attached a letter from the Director of
the Office of Management and Budget, which explained in some detail
the military operations that the additional budget would be used to fund.
Id. In December 2014, Congress passed the Consolidated and Further
Continuing Appropriations Acts of 2015, Pub. L. No. 113-235, 128 Stat
2130 (2014), in which it appropriated the funds the President had sought.

The President's proposed budget for 2016 also requested funds to
conduct Operation Inherent Resolve, and Congress again appropriated
the vast majority of the requested funds. Consolidated Appropriations
Act, 2016, Public L. No. 114-113, 129 Stat. 2242 (2015). . . .

. . . [T]he Court can discern no impasse or conflict between the
political branches on the question of whether ISIL is an appropriate
target under the AUMFs cited by the President as authority for Operation
Inherent Resolve.

This lack of conflict is relevant to the *justiciability* of Plaintiff's
claims under the political question doctrine because judicial intervention
into military affairs is particularly inappropriate when the two political
branches to whom war-making powers are committed are not in dispute
as to the military action at issue. *See U.S. ex rel. New v. Rumsfeld*, 350 F.
Supp. 2d 80, 97 (D.D.C. 2004), *aff'd*, 448 F.3d 403 (D.C. Cir. 2006)
("Petitioner raises a question of the allocation of war-making power
between the political branches . . . . There is, however, no conflict
between the branches on this matter . . . . When no evidence of such a
dispute even exists and, by all appearances, the executive and legislative
branches agreed in this instance that there was no need for congressional
approval, it would be most inappropriate for the Court to 'undertak[e]
independent resolution [of the issue] without expressing lack of the
respect due coordinate branches of government.'") (quoting *Baker*, 369

---

12. Letter from President Obama to the Speaker of the House of
Representatives (Nov. 10, 2014), https://www.whitehouse.gov/sites/default/files/
omb/assets/budget_amendments/amendment_11_10_14.pdf.

U.S. at 217); *Zivotofsky*, 132 S. Ct. at 1433 (Sotomayor, J., concurring) ("[I]t may be appropriate for courts to stay their hand in cases implicating delicate questions concerning the distribution of political authority between coordinate branches until a dispute is ripe, intractable, and incapable of resolution by the political process."); *Goldwater v. Carter*, 444 U.S. 996 (1979) (Powell, J., concurring) ("The Judicial Branch should not decide issues affecting the allocation of power between the President and Congress until the political branches reach a constitutional impasse.").

. . . Congress is vested with considerable power to restrain the President in the conduct of military operations. *See Schneider*, 412 F.3d at 198 ("If the executive in fact has exceeded his appropriate role in the constitutional scheme, Congress enjoys a broad range of authorities with which to exercise restraint and balance," including withholding funding); *Massachusetts v. Laird*, 451 F.2d at 34 ("When the executive takes a strong hand, Congress has no lack of corrective power."); *Ange v. Bush*, 752 F. Supp. 509, 514 (D.D.C. 1990) ("Congress possesses ample powers under the Constitution to prevent Presidential overreaching, should Congress choose to exercise them."). Such powers may not always be sufficient, and judicial intervention may be necessary when they fail. But in this case, where these powers have not been exercised and there does not appear to be any disagreement between the two political branches as to the legality of a live military operation, the Court finds it inappropriate to inject itself into these affairs. In sum, the Court finds that dismissal under the political question doctrine is appropriate.

Accordingly, the Court will dismiss Plaintiff's claims for two independent reasons. First, Plaintiff lacks standing. The "injuries" upon which Plaintiff grounds his claims do not constitute "injury in fact" as required to support Article III standing. Second, Plaintiff's claims raise non-justiciable political questions. This case raises questions that are committed to the political branches of government. The Court is not well-equipped to resolve these questions, and the political branches who are so-equipped do not appear to be in dispute as to their answers. . . .

––––––––––––––––

[NSL p. 409. Insert new Note 4.1.]

4.1. *Trump Administration Military Actions in Syria.* Shortly after taking office, the Trump administration published the following memorandum. As of early July 2017, the plan it prescribes had not been made public.

National Security Presidential Memorandum/NSPM-3, Plan to Defeat the Islamic State of Iraq and Syria

Jan. 28, 2017

The Islamic State of Iraq and Syria, or ISIS, is not the only threat from radical Islamic terrorism that the United States faces, but it is among the most vicious and aggressive. It is also attempting to create its own state, which ISIS claims as a "caliphate." But there can be no accommodation or negotiation with it. For those reasons I am directing my Administration to develop a comprehensive plan to defeat ISIS. . . .

ISIS has engaged in a systematic campaign of persecution and extermination in those territories it enters or controls. If ISIS is left in power, the threat that it poses will only grow. We know it has attempted to develop chemical weapons capability. It continues to radicalize our own citizens, and its attacks against our allies and partners continue to mount. The United States must take decisive action to defeat ISIS.

Sec. 1. Policy.

It is the policy of the United States that ISIS be defeated. . . .

Sec. 3. Plan to Defeat ISIS.

(a) Scope and Timing.

(i) Development of a new plan to defeat ISIS (the Plan) shall commence immediately.

(ii) Within 30 days, a preliminary draft of the Plan to defeat ISIS shall be submitted to the President by the Secretary of Defense.

(iii) The Plan shall include:

(A) a comprehensive strategy and plans for the defeat of ISIS;

(B) recommended changes to any United States rules of engagement and other United States policy restrictions that exceed the requirements of international law regarding the use of force against ISIS;

(C) public diplomacy, information operations, and cyber strategies to isolate and delegitimize ISIS and its radical Islamist ideology;

(D) identification of new coalition partners in the fight

against ISIS and policies to empower coalition partners to fight ISIS and its affiliates;

(E) mechanisms to cut off or seize ISIS's financial support, including financial transfers, money laundering, oil revenue, human trafficking, sales of looted art and historical artifacts, and other revenue sources; and

(F) a detailed strategy to robustly fund the Plan. . . .

Donald J. Trump

Is Congress entitled to see the new plan? Are members of the public? To what extent, if any, may Congress suspend or regulate implementation of any aspect of the plan by the President? What is the significance of changes recommended in Sec. 3(a)(iii)(B)?

Since late January 2017, U.S. forces have carried out thousands of air strikes against ISIS targets inside Syria. These actions are reported daily on the website of the Defense Department's Central Command, http://www.centcom.mil/MEDIA/PRESS-RELEASES/. In addition, by spring 2017 nearly 1,000 U.S. ground troops were deployed inside Syria, including some 500 Special Operations personnel, 250 Army Rangers, and 200 Marines. They were engaged in training, advice, and support for Kurdish and Arab fighters attacking ISIS. Deployment of another 1,000 conventional troops there was under consideration. See Thomas Gibbons-Neff, *U.S. Military Likely to Send as Many as 1,000 More Ground Troops into Syria Ahead of Raqqa Offensive, Officials Say*, Wash. Post, Mar. 15, 2017.

On April 4, 2017, Syrian forces conducted an attack against a target in northern Syria using chemical weapons — possibly sarin gas — killing dozens of civilians. In response, President Trump ordered the bombardment two days later of Syria's Shayrat Airfield using 59 Tomahawk cruise missiles launched from U.S. warships in the Mediterranean. (President Obama had threatened a military response when Assad used chemical weapons against Syrian civilians in 2013.) This unprecedented direct attack on Syrian forces was immediately condemned as unconstitutional and a violation of U.N. Charter Article 2(4), *see, e.g.*, Marty Lederman, *Why the Strikes Against Syria Probably Violate the U.N. Charter and (Therefore) the U.S. Constitution*, Just Security, Apr. 6, 2017, or excused as an act of humanitarian intervention in exercise of every nation's responsibility to protect (see casebook p. 484). *See, e.g.*, Harold Hongju Koh, *Not Illegal: But Now The Hard Part*

Begins, Just Security, Apr. 7, 2017. Did the U.S. strike violate either domestic or international law?

Following a more recent Pentagon report of "active preparations" by Syria for a renewed use of chemical weapons, the Trump administration warned that Syria would "pay a heavy price" if it used those weapons again. *See* Michael D. Shear, Helene Cooper & Eric Schmitt, *Syria Will "Pay a Heavy Price" for Another Chemical Attack, White House Says*, N.Y. Times, June 26, 2017. Was the President's threat lawful?

On May 18, 2017, U.S. warplanes attacked a pro-Assad military convoy as it approached a base in southern Syria where American and British personnel were training and advising Syrian rebels battling the Islamic State. According to U.S. officials, the purpose of the strike was to protect coalition forces, not to directly attack the Assad regime. *See* Eric Schmitt & Anne Barnard, *U.S. Warplanes in Syria Hit Pro-Government Militia Convoy*, N.Y. Times, May 18, 2017. But both Syria and Russia condemned the strike as a further illegal act of aggression, asserting that the United States had no right either to establish a base inside Syria or to defend it without Syrian permission. *See* Anne Barnard, *Russia and Syria Denounce U.S. Airstrike on Pro-Assad Militia*, N.Y. Times, May 19, 2017. The Trump administration claimed domestic authority under the 2001 AUMF. As a matter of international law, the U.S. military action was said to be a legitimate act of self-defense of its troops legally deployed inside Syria. Was either claim justified? *See* Tess Bridgeman, *About that "Deconfliction Zone" in Syria: Is the United States on Firm Domestic and International Legal Footing?*, Just Security, June 15, 2017.

On June 18, 2017, a U.S. fighter jet shot down a Syrian warplane that the United States claimed was attacking Syrian Democratic Forces, which has fought both ISIS and Syrian government forces. In response, Russia suspended the use of a U.S. hotline designed to avoid inadvertent clashes, and it threatened to shoot down any U.S. aircraft flying over Syria west of the Euphrates River. Michael R. Gordon & Ivan Nechepurenko, *Russia Warns U.S. After Downing of Syrian Warplane*, N.Y. Times, June 19, 2017. Does this development suggest the desirability of explicit congressional authorization for U.S. military actions inside Syria?

[NSL p. 409. Insert at the end of Note 5.]

S.J. RES. 43
115th Congress, 1st Session
May 25, 2017

JOINT RESOLUTION . . .

Sec. 3. Authorization for use of United States Armed Forces to prevent future acts of international terrorism against the United States.

(a) Authorization. — In order to prevent any future acts of international terrorism against the United States, the President is authorized to use all necessary and appropriate force against —
    (1) al-Qaeda and the Taliban;
    (2) the Islamic State of Iraq and Syria (also known as the Islamic State of Iraq and the Levant, the Islamic State, Daesh, ISIS, and ISIL); and
    (3) associated persons or forces as provided in section 4.
(b) War Powers Resolution requirements. —
    (1) Specific Statutory Authorization. — Consistent with section 8(a)(1) of the War Powers Resolution (50 U.S.C. 1547(a)(1)), Congress declares that this section is intended to constitute specific statutory authorization within the meaning of section 5(b) of the War Powers Resolution (50 U.S.C. 1544(b)). . . .

Sec. 4. Associated persons or forces.

(a) Associated persons and forces. — For purposes of section 3(a)(3), the term "associated persons or forces" means any person or force, other than a sovereign nation, that —
    (1) is a part of, or substantially supports al-Qaeda, the Taliban, or the Islamic State of Iraq and Syria; and
    (2) is engaged in hostilities against the United States, its Armed Forces, or its other personnel.
(b) Initial associated persons or forces. —
    (1) in General. — For purposes of section 3(a)(3), the term "associated persons or forces" includes any person or force meeting the definition in subsection (a) that is specified in the report under

paragraph (2).

(2) Report. — Not later than 60 days after the date of the enactment of this joint resolution, the President shall submit to Congress a report specifying the persons or forces (other than the groups al-Nusra Front (also known as Jabhat al-Nusra and Jabhat Fateh al-Sham), Khorasan Group, al-Qaeda in the Arabian Peninsula, and al-Shabaab, which Congress considers to be associated persons or forces for purposes of this joint resolution) that are associated persons or forces under subsection (a) as of the date of the enactment of this joint resolution.

(3) Disapproval. — The treatment of persons or forces specified in the report under paragraph (2) as associated persons or forces under subsection (a) is subject to disapproval in accordance with section 6.

(c) Additional associated persons or forces. — [providing similarly for subsequent notification and possible disapproval by Congress] . . .

Sec. 5. Countries in which operations authorized.

Subject to disapproval in accordance with section 6, the use of force authorized by section 3 may take place in a country (other than Afghanistan, Iraq, Syria, Somalia, Libya, or Yemen) if the President submits to Congress a report on the use of force in such country that includes the following;

(1) The name of the country in which the use of force will take place.

(2) A description of the presence in the country of al-Qaeda, the Taliban, or the Islamic State of Iraq and Syria, or associated persons or forces currently covered by section 4.

(3) A justification why the use of force in the country is necessary and appropriate.

Sec. 6. Expedited procedures for joint resolution of disapproval of use of force against initial or additional associated persons or forces or in other countries. [setting forth detailed procedures in both Houses for prompt consideration of a resolution of disapproval] . . .

Sec. 7. Effect of enactment of joint resolution of disapproval of use of force against initial or additional associated persons or forces or in other countries. [providing for suspension of previously authorized use of force] . . .

Sec. 8. Duration of authorization.

(a) In general. — In order to encourage periodic review of the use of force authorized by this joint resolution, the authorization for use of force in section 3 shall terminate five years after the date of the enactment of this joint resolution, unless reauthorized by Congress. . . .

Sec. 9. Repeal of Authorization for Use of Military Force.

The Authorization for Use of Military Force (Public Law 107-40; 50 U.S.C. 1541 note) [enacted September 18, 2001] is repealed, effective 60 days after the date of the enactment of this joint resolution.

Sec. 10. Repeal of Authorization for Use of Military Force Against Iraq Resolution of 2002.

The Authorization for Use of Military Force Against Iraq Resolution of 2002 (Public Law 107-243; 50 U.S.C. 1541 note) [enacted October 16, 2002] is repealed, effective 60 days after the date of the enactment of this joint resolution. . . .

Sec. 12. Reports to Congress.

(a) Strategy. — Not later than 90 days after the date of the enactment of this joint resolution, the President shall submit to the appropriate committees and leadership of Congress a report setting forth a comprehensive strategy of the United States, encompassing military, economic, humanitarian, and diplomatic capabilities, to protect the United States from al-Qaeda, the Taliban, and the Islamic State of Iraq and Syria in their fight to defeat such organizations.

(b) Implementation of strategy. — [requiring detailed periodic reports to Congress on implementation of the strategy and substantive changes in strategy] . . . .

_____

S.J. Res. 43, co-sponsored by Senators Tim Kaine (D-Va.) and Jeff Flake (R-Ariz.), clearly represents a bipartisan effort to exercise greater congressional oversight and control over the ongoing use of military force against terrorists. Does it follow the scholars' recommendations for such legislation outlined above? Does it reflect the Framers' concern that unilateral presidential uses of force could precipitate a wider conflict? Or does it unconstitutionally infringe on the President's prerogatives as Commander in Chief? What amendments to the resolution would you recommend? *See* Ryan Goodman, *Important Features of Senators Kaine and Flake's Proposed War Authorization for ISIS — with Annotations*, Just Security, May 25, 2017. Why do you suppose Congress will likely take no action on the proposal?

[NSL p. 409. Insert new Note 6.]

6. *Expanding the Battlefield.* The United States has long deployed troops equipped for combat in locations where it was not engaged in a "war," but where U.S. interests were said to be threatened. During the Reagan administration, for example, U.S. forces were sent to El Salvador as "advisors" (see casebook p. 359), and U.S. aircraft flew combat missions over Serbia during the Clinton administration (see casebook p. 360). More recently, American military forces have carried out attacks against Al Qaeda or ISIS targets in Libya, Yemen, and Somalia, and they have served as trainers and advisors elsewhere.

In 2017, President Trump declared parts of Yemen and Somalia to be areas of "active hostilities," formally approving U.S. offensive military actions in those places and suspending the operation of Obama-era rules designed to limit civilian casualties outside of conventional war zones. *See* Charlie Savage & Eric Schmitt, *Trump Eases Rules in Somalia Protecting Civilians in Strikes*, N.Y. Times, Mar. 31, 2017; Charlie Savage, Helene Cooper & Eric Schmitt, *With New Rules in Place, U.S. Strikes the Shabab*, N.Y. Times, June 12, 2017.

How, if at all, do these declarations affect the 2013 *U.S. Policy Standards and Procedures for the Use of Force in Counterterrorism Operations Outside the United States and Areas of Active Hostilities*, set out at casebook p. 425? International humanitarian law implications of the changes in rules are examined in this *Supplement, infra* pp. 27-28. Are the changes tactical or strategic? Do they alter domestic authority for U.S. military actions in the two countries?

[NSL p. 427, CTL p. 149. Insert before Note 1.]

0. *Presidential Policy Guidance.* A partially redacted version of a Presidential Policy Guidance titled "Procedures for Approving Direct Action Against Terrorist Targets Located Outside the United States and

Areas of Active Hostilities" was released by the Obama Administration in March 2016. It is available at https://www.aclu.org/sites/default/files/field_document/presidential_policy_guidance.pdf. The U.S. Policy Standards excerpted in the casebook were a summary of this much more detailed document. The Presidential Policy Guidance is generally consistent with that summary, but it clarifies that so-called "signature strikes" are not always directed against persons whose identity is unknown; they may also be directed at military targets such as improvised explosive devices and explosives storage facilities. *Id.* §4.A.

Although the Policy Guidance provides an unprecedented look at what has been characterized as an "extraordinarily detailed and comprehensive" interagency and interbranch review process for the use of force, *see* Marty Lederman, *The Presidential Policy Guidance for Targeting and Capture Outside Afghanistan, Iraq and Syria*, Lawfare, Aug. 6, 2016 (suggesting that it may be the basis for rumored concerns about presidential "micromanagement" of the military), it has still been criticized by human rights organizations for insufficient transparency. *See* Columbia Law School Human Rights Clinic and Sana'a Center for Strategic Studies, *Out of the Shadows* (June 2017).

[NSL p. 428, CTL p. 150. Insert after Note 7.]

7.1. *Relaxation of Combat Rules.* In 2017, President Trump reportedly exempted Somalia from the Obama administration's 2013 U.S. Policy Standards, permitting the U.S. military to strike suspected Somali Shabab fighters based strictly on their combatant status, instead of the threat they pose to Americans. *See* Charlie Savage & Eric Schmidt, *Trump Eases Combat Rules in Somalia Intended to Protect Civilians*, N.Y. Times, Mar. 30, 2017. The new rules also lifted the "near-certainty" standard for collateral damage. They now permit U.S. military activities to be conducted under the more lenient default IHL standards, which allow collateral damage if it is necessary and proportionate. *Id.* Nevertheless, the head of the U.S. Africa Command said that he had decided to keep the near-certainty standard for now. *Id.*

A strike under the new rules on a Shabab training camp in March 2017 reportedly killed more than 150 people, described by U.S. officials as newly minted Shabab fighters attending a graduation ceremony. Charlie Savage, Helene Cooper & Eric Schmidt, *U.S. Strikes Shabab, Likely a First Since Trump Relaxed Rules for Somalia,* N.Y. Times, June 11, 2017.

7.2. *Congressional Oversight?* The National Defense Authorization Act for Fiscal Year 2017 requires the Secretary of Defense to notify the congressional defense committees of "sensitive military operations" within 48 hours after an operation. A *sensitive military operation* is

> (1) A lethal operation or capture operation —
> (A) conducted by the armed forces outside a declared theater of active armed conflict; or
> (B) conducted by a foreign partner in coordination with the armed forces that targets a specific individual or individuals.
> (2) An operation conducted by the armed forces outside a declared theater of active armed conflict in self-defense or in defense of foreign partners, including during a cooperative operation. [10 U.S.C. §130f(d) (Supp. IV 2016).]

Would this notification requirement apply to a lethal operation in Nigeria by a Nigerian military unit against suspected members of the militant Islamist group, Boko Haram, if U.S. military authorities provide reconnaissance for the operation? How do you think this notification requirement might influence the use of targeted killings by the U.S. military?

[NSL p. 443, CTL p. 165. Insert after Note 7.]

7.1. *The "Drone Memos."* Documents from the Obama Administration concerning targeted killing are compiled in *The Drone Memos* (Jameel Jaffer ed., The New Press 2016).

[NSL p. 458. Insert at the end of Note 8.]

The second edition of the *Tallinn Manual* was released in 2017, *Tallinn Manual 2.0 on the International Law Applicable to Cyber Operations. Tallinn Manual 2.0* extends its coverage of the international law governing cyber warfare to peacetime legal regimes. Included are sections covering sovereignty, state responsibility, human rights, and the law of air, space, and the sea. In addition, the new *Manual* adds to the first edition treatment of *jus ad bellum* rules on the use of force and *jus in bello* principles in the law of armed conflict.

[NSL p. 463. Insert at the end of Note 3.]

In late 2011, Congress enacted this provision in the National Defense Authorization Act for FY2012, Pub. L. No. 112-81, 125 Stat. 1298 (codified at 10 U.S.C. §111 note):

Sec. 954. Military Activities in Cyberspace.

Congress affirms that the Department of Defense has the capability, and upon direction by the President may conduct offensive operations in cyberspace to defend our Nation, Allies and interests, subject to —
(1) the policy principles and legal regimes that the Department follows for kinetic capabilities, including the law of armed conflict; and
(2) the War Powers Resolution (50 U.S.C. 1541 et seq.).

Does this provision confer authority on the military that it did not have before? Is so, how would you describe the scope of that authority? Can you think of other limitations that should have been listed in the provision? The legislative history confirms that a House bill would have clarified that the military has the authority to conduct clandestine cyberspace activities in support of military operations conducted pursuant to the 2001 AUMF outside the United States or to defend against a cyber attack on an asset of the Department of Defense. The conferees retained the language above that had been approved by the Senate. *Conference Report on H.R. 1540, National Defense Authorization Act for Fiscal Year 2012*, 157 Cong. Rec. H8356, H8599-8600 (Dec. 12, 2011).

On May 11, 2017, President Trump signed Exec. Order No. 13,800, *Strengthening the Cybersecurity of Federal Networks and Critical Infrastructure*, 82 Fed. Reg. 22,391. The order requires improvements in cybersecurity risk management and IT modernization in the executive branch, including requiring agency heads to be guided by the National Institute for Standards and Technology (NIST) *Framework for Improving Critical Infrastructure Cybersecurity* (Feb. 12, 2014). The order also promises federal support for owners and operators of critical infrastructure. Finally, the order requires federal agencies to report on options for better security for the Internet and for supporting the growth of a cybersecurity-trained workforce.

[NSL p. 510, CTL p. 186. Insert before "Notes and Questions."]

On April 4, 2017, President Trump signed National Security Presidential Memorandum-4, *Organization of the National Security Council, the Homeland Security Council, and Subcommittees*, https://assets.documentcloud.org/documents/3536323/2017-07064.pdf. The April memorandum significantly revised a January 2017 memorandum which had dramatically changed the historic structure, membership, and processes of the NSC. As revised, NSPM-4 parallels the structure utilized in the Obama administration. The agenda of NSC meetings is determined by the National Security Advisor, currently Lt. Gen. H.R. McMaster. NSPM-4 also restores the DNI, CIA Director, and Chairman of the Joint Chiefs of Staff as regular attendees of NSC meetings. The revised memorandum also removes the President's Chief Strategist from the list of invitees to NSC meetings and Principals Committee meetings. NSPM-4 also provides the same structure for the Deputies Committee and Policy Coordinating Committees as during the Obama administration.

[NSL p. 532. Insert at the end of Note 2.]

In the final days of the Obama administration, a series of releases by the ODNI and additional agencies within the Intelligence Community sought to provide greater transparency to the processes of intelligence collection, retention, and dissemination. Among the releases on January 12, 2017 was *Procedures for the Availability or Dissemination of Raw Signals Intelligence Information by the National Security Agency under Section 2.3 of Executive Order 12333*, https://www.dni.gov/files/documents/icotr/RawSIGINTGuidelines-as-approved-redacted.pdf.

In a nutshell, the *Raw SIGINT Availability Procedures* outline the process that intelligence agencies must follow for requesting, protecting, processing, retaining, disseminating, oversight, and legal use of "any SIGINT . . . that has not been evaluated for foreign intelligence purposes and/or minimized." *Id.* at 20. The procedures do not apply to SIGINT activities conducted by the NSA under §1.7(c)(2) of Exec. Order No. 12,333, SIGINT collected by the NSA under the Foreign Intelligence Surveillance Act (see NSL Chapter 23), or collection activities of any kind.

Under Exec. Order No. 12,333, CIA's collection, retention, and dissemination of information concerning U.S. persons are governed by procedures approved by the Director of the CIA and the Attorney General, after consultation with the Director of National Intelligence. The CIA AG Guidelines had not been significantly updated since 1982. In the intervening decades, CIA implemented a number of additional changes in internal regulations and policies to address changes in law and technology not contemplated in the 1980s. On January 18, 2017, CIA released its new, consolidated CIA AG Guidelines, in entirely unredacted form, at least in part due to the recognition by CIA that in the digital age, significant incidental collection of U.S. person data is bound to occur. *Central Intelligence Agency Intelligence Activities: Procedures Approved by the Attorney General Pursuant to Executive Order 12333* (Jan. 18, 2017), https://www.cia.gov/about-cia/privacy-and-civil-liberties/CIA-AG-Guidelines-Signed.pdf. *See* John Reed, *The CIA's New Guidelines for Handling Americans' Information*, Just Security, Jan. 18, 2017; Jennifer Daskal, *Five Quick Observation: The CIA's New Guidelines for Handling Americans' Data*, Just Security, Jan. 19, 2017.

[NSL p. 538. Insert at the end of Note 6.]

The funds appropriated for U.S. intelligence increased in 2016 by about five percent to a total of $70.7 billion, up from a combined total of $66.8 billion for the NIP and MIP in 2015. *Intelligence Spending Increased in 2016*, Secrecy News, Oct. 31, 2016.

[NSL p. 541. Insert new Note 12.]

12. *Historical Transparency at the CIA*. The CIA has posted its CREST (CIA Records Research Tool) database of more than 11 million pages of historical CIA records that have been declassified and approved for public release. The database may be accessed here: https://www.cia.gov/library/readingroom/collection/crest-25-year-program-archive.

[NSL p. 606, CTL p. 234. Insert at the end of Note 6.]

The en banc Second Circuit affirmed in *United States v. Ganias*, 824 F.3d 199 (2d Cir. 2016) (en banc). The Supreme Court denied certiorari. *See Ganias v. United States*, 137 S. Ct. 569 (2016) (mem.).

[NSL p. 621, CTL p. 249. Insert after Note 5.]

6. *Cell-Tower Locational Data: Another Frontier?* At this writing, the Supreme Court has granted certiorari in *United States v. Carpenter*, 819 F.3d 880 (6th Cir. 2016), *cert. granted*, No. 16-402, 2017 WL 2407484 (U.S. June 5, 2017), in which the court of appeals rejected a Fourth Amendment challenge to the prosecution's use of historical cell-tower locational data to convict the defendant. The case provides another opportunity for the Supreme Court to discuss the impact of new technology on Fourth Amendment protections. See *infra* this *Supplement* pp. 45-46.

[NSL, p. 645, CTL p. 273. Insert at the end of Note 3.]

As noted at p. 37 in this *Supplement*, *supra*, under Exec. Order No. 12,333, CIA's collection, retention, and dissemination of information concerning U.S. persons are governed by procedures approved by the Director of the CIA and the Attorney General, after consultation with the Director of National Intelligence. The CIA AG Guidelines had not been significantly updated since 1982. In the intervening decades, CIA implemented a number of additional changes in internal regulations and policies to address changes in law and technology not contemplated in the 1980s. On January 18, 2017, CIA released new, consolidated CIA AG Guidelines, in an entirely unredacted form, at least in part due to the recognition by CIA that in the digital age, significant incidental collection of U.S. person data is bound to occur. *Central Intelligence Agency Intelligence Activities: Procedures Approved by the Attorney General Pursuant to Executive Order 12333* (Jan. 18, 2017), https://www.cia.gov/about-cia/privacy-and-civil-liberties/CIA-AG-Guidelines-Signed.pdf.

[NSL p. 660, CTL p. 288. Add a new paragraph at the end of C. FISA TRENDS.]

The ODNI website and annual transparency reports on FISA and other intelligence authorities continued to provide information on activities of the FISC and FISCR. In 2016, the FISC issued 1,559 "probable cause" orders, directed at an estimated 1,687 targets. Of the targets, 19.9 percent were U.S. persons. An additional reporting requirement was added by statute in 2015. The USA FREEDOM Act, 50 U.S.C. §1873, requires the Administrative Office of the United States Courts to provide annual reports on the activities of the FISA courts. Its first annual report, for 2016, provides additional details on the activities of the FISC. Letter from James C. Duff, Director, Admin. Off. of the U.S. Courts, to Bob Goodlatte, Chairman, H. Comm. on the Judiciary (Apr. 20, 2017). For example, the report indicates that 78 percent of the applications to the FISC were granted as requested, 19 percent were granted after modifications by the court to the government's proposed order, and about two percent were denied in part — the court granted some authorities or targets requested but not others — and a few were denied in full. Additional aspects of the reports will be examined in the next two chapters. The report is available here: https://lawfareblog.com/ 2016-fisa-court-report-released.

[NSL, p. 701. CTL p. 329. Insert new Note 3(e).]

(e) *Queries of Raw Section 702 Data Using U.S.-Person Identifiers*. Do queries by the FBI using U.S.-person identifiers of raw data collected pursuant to Section 702 in non-national security criminal investigations constitute a "search"? Not long after enactment of the FAA, Senator Ron Wyden and others began to warn of a "backdoor search loophole" that could be used for warrantless surveillance of American citizens. Elizabeth Goitein, *The FBI's Warrantless Surveillance Back Door Just Opened a Little Wider*, Just Security, Apr. 21, 2016.

In April 2017 the ODNI declassified for release a redacted November 6, 2015 FISC opinion by Judge Thomas Hogan concluding that FBI queries in non-national security investigations are not searches. https://www.dni.gov/files/documents/20151106- 702Mem_Opinion_Order_for_Public_Release.pdf. Rather than reviewing the constitutionality of the queries of collected data, the FISC determined to assess the Fourth Amendment reasonableness of the 702

scheme "viewed as a whole." If the constitutional reasonableness of 702
turns on the recognition of a foreign intelligence exception to the
Warrant Clause, how can the same analysis support queries of collected
data in non-national security criminal investigations? Although critics
worried about the scale of the potential privacy invasion through the
"backdoor searches," the *Intelligence Community Statistical
Transparency Report Regarding the Use of National Security Authorities
for Calendar Year 2016,* https://icontherecord.tumblr.com/
transparency/odni_transparencyreport_cy2016, concludes that the
number of such queries in non-national security investigations for 2016
was one. Adam Klein, *Today's Big News About "Backdoor Searches,"*
Lawfare, May 2, 2017.

In contrast, other agencies, primarily the NSA and CIA, used 5,288
search terms associated with Americans in national security
investigations. Charlie Savage, *Fight Brews Over Push to Shield
Americans in Warrantless Surveillance,* N.Y. Times, May 6, 2017. The
2017 legislative consideration of FAA reauthorization is ongoing at this
writing. Proposed statutory criteria for querying collected data are among
the issues being debated. *Id.*

[NSL p. 703, CTL p. 331. Insert at the end of Note 7.]

On December 5, 2016, a panel of the Ninth Circuit affirmed
Mohamed Osman Mohamud's conviction for attempting to detonate a
large bomb during the annual Christmas tree lighting ceremony in
downtown Portland, Oregon. In the course of affirming the conviction,
the court held that incidental Section 702 acquisition of U.S. citizen
Mohamud's email communications during an investigation of a foreign
national abroad did not require a warrant and was not unreasonable under
the Fourth Amendment. *United States v. Mohamud,* 843 F.3d 420 (9th
Cir. 2016).

The court emphasized that it was ruling on "the particular facts of
this case," and it distinguished the apparent PRISM collection on
Mohamud from different analyses that might have been required if
Mohamud had been subject to upstream collection or to querying from a
database of collected communications. Mohamud argued that the
approach taken by the FISCR in *In re Directives,* 551 F.3d 1004 (FISA
Ct. Rev. 2008) (NSL p. 609, CTL p. 237) — that "incidental collections
occurring as a result of constitutionally permissible acquisitions do not
render those acquisitions unlawful," *id.* at 1015 — should not be applied,

because his surveillance was not really "incidental" to the extent that investigators contemplated the acquisition of the U.S. person communications. The court answered that "[t]he fact that the government knew some U.S. persons' communications would be swept up during foreign intelligence gathering does not make such collection any more unlawful in this context than in the Title III or traditional FISA context." 843 F.3d at 440.

The panel did find "troubling" the scale of incidental collection, which it characterized as "vast, not *de minimus*," thus distinguishing §702 collection from Title III and traditional FISA. *Id.* However, based on a reduced but not clearly specified privacy interest Mohamud had in the contents of emails to or from a foreign person located outside the United States, the collection was constitutional. The court also noted that the volume of U.S. person collection does "increase the importance of minimization procedures once the communications are collected." *Id.*

In a civil challenge to the constitutionality of §702 upstream collection, on May 23, 2017 the Fourth Circuit reversed a district court decision and held that the Wikimedia Foundation had standing to sue the NSA. *Wikimedia Found. v. NSA*, 857 F.3d 193 (4th Cir. 2017). In contrast to the plaintiffs in *Clapper v. Amnesty International USA*, 568 U.S. 398 (2013) (NSL p. 145), the Fourth Circuit held that, if taken as true, the allegations of injury by Wikimedia resulting from upstream were not speculative — and thus were sufficient to survive a motion to dismiss on standing grounds. (Recall that the *Clapper* case reached the Supreme Court at the summary judgment stage of litigation — by which point the plaintiffs must have adduced evidence tending to support their allegations.)

In essence, Wikimedia argued that the sheer volume of its communications, coupled with the NSA practice of upstream collection of substantial quantities of text-based communications entering and leaving the United States, makes it virtually certain that NSA is collecting at least some of its communications — thus creating an injury sufficient to support its First and Fourth Amendments claims. The court agreed. In contrast to *Clapper,* where the arguable standing was based on prospective or threatened injury, Wikimedia's allegations were for an actual, ongoing injury, caused by the defendants and remediable by the court. Over a partial dissent from Judge Davis, however, the court affirmed the dismissal of a more general "dragnet theory" challenge to Section 702 by other public interest and media plaintiffs in the same suit, concluding that the other plaintiffs had not pleaded sufficient facts that would, if true, support their claim that the NSA is "intercepting, copying, and reviewing substantially all" text-based communications entering and leaving the United States. *See* 857 F.3d at 213.

[NSL p. 704, CTL p. 332. Insert new Notes.]

3. *Ending Upstream "About" Collection.* Under Section 702, the NSA was collecting not just "to/from" communications, but also "about" communications that contained references to the name of a tasked account, described in Judge Bates' 2011 FISC opinion, *supra*. Recall that Judge Bates ruled that because "about" collection was resulting in the NSA's acquisition of tens of thousands of purely domestic emails each year, the practice violated the Fourth Amendment. Judge Bates then approved revised NSA procedures to deal with "about " and other collection of domestic communications two months later. *See* Note 1, *supra*. In essence, the revised rules prohibited NSA analysts from searching for U.S.-person information within collected upstream data.

On April 28, 2017, the NSA announced that it is no longer collecting emails and texts exchanged by U.S. persons with persons abroad that simply mention identifying terms for foreign targets, but that are neither to or from those targets. *NSA Stops Certain Section 702 "Upstream" Activities*, https://www.nsa.gov/news-features/press-room/press-releases/2017/nsa-stops-certain-702-activites.shtml. The announcement came after it was revealed that NSA analysts had violated the minimization procedures approved by the FISC in November 2011. Charlie Savage, *N.S.A. Halts Collection of Americans' Emails About Foreign Targets*, N.Y. Times, Apr. 28, 2017. The NSA explained that it had reported the compliance problems to the FISC, but called its failures to comply with the rules approved by the FISC "inadvertent." The FISC had issued short-term extensions of the program while NSA examined whether it could continue collecting information on targets without violating the minimization rules. *Id.*

Why would NSA have decided to end "about" collection without being ordered to do so by a court? Can you predict the net intelligence losses and privacy gains likely to occur as a result of ending "about" collection?

Recall that the PRISM or "downstream" collection program does not collect "about" communications. Nor does the end of upstream "about" collection affect surveillance that occurs abroad, where most intelligence collection is governed by Exec. Order No. 12,333.

4. *Continuing Procedural Changes and FISC Activity*. On September 26, 2016, the NSA submitted certifications to the FISC for reauthorization of its targeting and minimization procedures under 702. However, while the FISC review was being conducted, the NSA informed the FISC that there had been "significant noncompliance" with the procedures as submitted. *Foreign Intelligence Surveillance Court Approves New Targeting and Minimization Procedures: A Summary*, Lawfare, May 15, 2017. The NSA Inspector General report found that NSA analysts had been using U.S.-person identifiers to query upstream collection, in violation of the minimization procedures. The scope and extent of the abuses were not made public, although the IG reported that the problem was "widespread at all periods of review." *Id*. After reprimands from the FISC for the NSA's "lack of candor," and extensions of the FISC review period to permit NSA to bring itself into compliance, on March 30, 2017, the government submitted to the FISC revised targeting and minimization procedures for the NSA and FBI, and minimization procedures for the CIA and NCTC.

The NSA Minimization Procedures may be found here: https://www.dni.gov/files/documents/icotr/51117/2016-NSA-702-Minimization-Procedures_Mar_30_17.pdf.

The NSA Targeting Procedures are here: https://www.dni.gov/files/documents/icotr/51117/2016_NSA_702_Targeting_Procedures_Mar_30_17.pdf.

The FISC issued a lengthy memorandum order and opinion approving the new and amended targeting and minimization procedures on April 26, 2017. *See* https://www.dni.gov/files/documents/icotr/51117/2016_Cert_FISC_Memo_Opin_Order_Apr_2017.pdf. The court noted with approval the abandonment of "about" collection by NSA, and the resulting targeting procedures that restrict acquisitions "to communications to or from persons targeted in accordance with [the] procedures." *Id*. After considerable discussion, the court found that the newly revised NSA targeting and minimization procedures meet the requirements of the FAA and the Fourth Amendment.

Regarding the NCTC, the court approved a proposal that, for the first time, allows the NCTC to access unminimized information acquired by the NSA and FBI. Although NCTC does not have access to upstream data or telephony, the FISC was persuaded that "NCTC's role as the government's primary organization for analyzing and integrating all intelligence pertaining to international terrorism and counterterrorism" merits its *access* to the additional raw data. *Id*. The FISC allowed the NCTC to *retain* "raw" 702 information, however, only where it is determined to be evidence of a crime and "only as long as reasonably necessary to serve a law enforcement purpose." *Id.*

Pursuant to a FOIA request from the Electronic Frontier Foundation, in June 2017 the FISC released 18 redacted opinions regarding Section 702. In the main, the opinions concern the authorization of proposed targeting and minimization procedures and their consistency with the statute and the Fourth Amendment. Summaries of the opinions and a cover letter from the Civil Division of DOJ are available at Chris Mirasola & Yishai Schwartz, *The 18 FISA Court Opinions on Section 702: Summaries*, Lawfare, June 23, 2017.

5. *Reauthorization in 2017?* At this writing in July 2017, hearings had been held in the House and Senate on bills to reauthorize or revise the FISA Amendments Act in advance of its December 31, 2017 sunset. Several cross-cutting arguments and approaches to programmatic surveillance and its reform have been proposed, and the legislative outcome remains uncertain. Although a small group of Senators and Representatives seek a permanent reauthorization of the FAA, most members are focused on the utility of reforms that would arguably better protect privacy without sacrificing the needs of the intelligence community. The most likely candidates for reform include:

(a) Codifying the end of "about" collection. The dramatic April 2017 announcement by NSA that it would end the "about" aspect of upstream collection because of serious compliance problems changed the legislative odds. A ban on "about" collection would simply confirm what is now administrative practice.

(b) Limiting the use of Section 702 data by law enforcement. Allowing the FBI to use Section 702 data to investigate any federal crime risks serious Fourth Amendment threats in the future. Although the *Transparency Report, supra,* reported only one such search in 2016, the ODNI statistics do not include foreign intelligence-based searches that could generate criminal evidence. Nor do they predict future use. Because law enforcement use strays from the foreign intelligence purpose of FISA in general and Section 702, in particular, Congress may agree to prohibit (or more aggressively circumscribe) law enforcement use of Section 702 data.

(c) Limiting incidental collection on U.S. persons. So far, intelligence agencies have relied on minimization procedures to protect the privacy of U.S. persons whose communications are incidentally collected under Section 702. Although some members of Congress have asked the DNI and the NSA to publicly estimate the number of U.S.

person communications incidentally acquired under Section 702, the government has so far been unable to generate a reliable estimate. Without a good estimate of the numbers of Americans impacted by Section 702, it is difficult to predict limiting reforms. One approach under consideration is to specify targeting criteria focused on espionage, terrorism, and other security threats to the United States. Jake Laperruque, *How Congress Should Evaluate Section 702's Security Value When Debating Its Reauthorization*, Lawfare, June 16, 2017.

(d) Requiring judicial approval for U.S.-person queries. This issue is explored *supra*, pp. 39-40 in this *Supplement*. The government argues that it can currently query its databases quickly and efficiently to sort and identify communications already lawfully collected without having to sift through each individual communication. Moreover, it asserts, queries using U.S.-person identifiers are useful in detecting and evaluating any connections with U.S. persons and lawfully targeted foreign persons. The courts have so far sided with the government on this issue.

[NSL p. 719, CTL p. 347. Insert before "f. Telephony Metadata."]

In *United States v. Carpenter*, 819 F.3d 880 (6th Cir. 2016), *cert. granted,* No. 16-402, 2017 WL 2407484 (U.S. June 5, 2017), the Court of Appeals for the Sixth Circuit agreed with the Eleventh Circuit in rejecting the defendant's Fourth Amendment challenge to the prosecution's use of stored locational data created by defendant's cell phone. Judge Kethledge wrote that "for the same reasons that *Smith* had no expectation of privacy in the numerical information at issue there, the defendants have no such expectation in the locational information here. On this point, *Smith* is binding precedent." *Id.* at 888. Judge Stranch thought this issue harder, and therefore concurred only in the judgment on other grounds. *See id.* at 893-897 (Stranch, J., concurring in part and concurring in the judgment).

[NSL p. 721, CTL p. 349. Insert after Note 3.]

At this writing, the Supreme Court has granted certiorari in *United States v. Carpenter*, 819 F.3d 880 (6th Cir. 2016), *cert. granted,* No. 16-402, 2017 WL 2407484 (U.S. June 5, 2017), to consider "[w]hether the warrantless seizure and search of historical cell phone records revealing the location and movements of a cell phone user over the

course of 127 days is permitted by the Fourth Amendment." Petition for
a Writ of Certiorari at 1, *Carpenter*, No. 16-402. Given the lower court's
straightforward (mechanical?) application of the third-party doctrine and
the absence of a circuit split, the grant of certiorari has spurred
speculation that the Supreme Court will revisit that doctrine. *See, e.g.,*
Jordan Brunner, *Supreme Court Grants Cert in Carpenter v. United
States: An Overview*, Lawfare, Jun. 6, 2017 (noting that as of June 6,
2017, there had been eighteen separate majority, concurring, and
dissenting opinions across five circuit courts on this question).

_____

[NSL p. 737, CTL p. 365. Insert after Note 1.]

   1.1. *Extraterritoriality of SCA §2703(a)*. In its survey of government
information-gathering authority, the *Doe I* court mentions the Stored
Communications Act (SCA) authority to access the *contents* of recently
stored (less than 180 days) email by obtaining a search warrant on a
showing of probable cause under the Federal Rules of Criminal
Procedure. NSL p. 728, CTL p. 356. In *Microsoft v. United States*, 829
F.3d 197 (2d Cir. 2016), *petition for cert. filed*, No. 17-2 (U.S. June 23,
2017), the government had subpoenaed certain *non-content* subscriber
information stored by Microsoft in the United States in a criminal
investigation of suspected narcotics trafficking. Microsoft complied with
the subpoena. Using the SCA, however, the government had also
obtained a search warrant issued on probable cause for *content*
information for the same customer(s?) stored by Microsoft in Ireland.
When Microsoft refused to comply with the warrant, it was held in
contempt and then appealed.

   Applying the presumption against extraterritoriality (NSL p. 247),
the court of appeals held that the SCA's warrant provision was only
intraterritorial and therefore did not reach storage in Ireland. While the
Federal Rules of Criminal Procedure authorize a federal judge to issue a
warrant for a search outside her district, they only authorize such
warrants for searches in *other* districts, the court wrote, not for searches
outside the United States. 829 F.3d at 213. Judge Lynch wrote separately
to emphasize both why he believed that was the correct result under the
existing language of the SCA, and why Congress should amend the SCA
to override it. *See id.* at 231-233 (Lynch, J., concurring in the judgment).

   Of course, the fact that content information is stored in Ireland does
not mean that it can only be viewed there. Microsoft can read it in the
United States. Indeed, that's where the government would read it. Where

does the search of the customer's content information occur? Where does the invasion of the customer's privacy occur? What incentive does the *Microsoft* decision give providers of cloud storage who wish to protect their customers' content data from U.S. search warrants?

District courts in other circuits have rejected the *Microsoft* conclusion:

> Under the facts before this court, the conduct relevant to the SCA's focus will occur in the United States. That is, the invasions of privacy will occur in the United States; the searches of the electronic data disclosed by Google pursuant to the warrants will occur in the United States when the FBI reviews the copies of the requested data in Pennsylvania. These cases, therefore, involve a permissible domestic application of the SCA, even if other conduct (the electronic transfer of data) occurs abroad. [*In re Search Warrant No. 16–960–M–01 to Google*, No. 16-1061-M, 2017 WL 471564, at *11 (E.D. Pa. Feb. 3, 2017).]

The United States has filed a petition for a writ of certiorari in the *Microsoft* case, and various bills have been introduced in Congress that could override the Second Circuit decision in that case regardless of what happens before the Supreme Court.

[NSL p. 764, CTL p. 392. Insert at the end of Note 6.]

As noted in this *Supplement, supra* pp. 45-46, the Supreme Court's grant of certiorari in *United States v. Carpenter*, 819 F.3d 880 (6th Cir. 2016), *cert. granted,* No. 16-402, 2017 WL 2407484 (U.S. June 5, 2017), may portend a reconsideration of the third-party doctrine. Although the case only presents the question of its application to historical cell-tower locational data, it could have ramifications for bulk collection of metadata as well.

[NSL p. 768, CTL p. 396. Insert after Note 1.]

1.1. *Use of bulk collection.* The Office of the Director of National Intelligence (ODNI) reported that in 2016 the FISC issued 84 orders under its §1861(2)(B) authority, with 88 targets and 81,035 unique identifiers, as well as 40 orders for call detail records (telephony metadata) under its §1861(2)(C) authority, with 42 targets, generating 151,230,968 call detail records, which it queried with 22,360 search terms. ODNI, *Statistical Transparency Report Regarding the Use of National Security Authorities for Calendar Year 2016* (*ODNI Transparency Report*), *available at* https://icontherecord.tumblr.com/transparency/odni_transparencyreport_cy2016. The ODNI explained the size of the number of call detail records as follows:

> As an example, assume an NSA intelligence analyst learns that phone number (202) 555-1234 is being used by a suspected international terrorist. This is the "specific selection term" or "selector" that will be submitted to the FISC (or the Attorney General in an emergency) for approval using the "reasonable articulable suspicion" (RAS) standard. Assume that one provider (provider X) submits to NSA a record showing (202) 555-1234 had called (301) 555-4321 on May 1, 2016. This is the "first hop" and would count as one record. If the provider submits records showing additional calls between those same telephone numbers, each would count as an additional record. Thus, if over the course of 2016, (202) 555-1234 was in contact with (301) 555-4321 once each day, then that would count as 365 records obtained from provider X. If another provider (provider Y) also submits records showing direct contact between those two telephone numbers (assume the same number of contacts), then those would add to the count.
>
> In turn, assume that NSA submits the "first-hop" number above — (301) 555-4321 — to the providers, and finds that it was used to call (410) 555-5678. This is the "second-hop" result. Each contact between the first-hop and second-hop numbers would count as a separate record, as would each such contact submitted by other providers. [*Id.*]

[NSL p. 768, CTL p. 396. Insert after Note 2.]

2.1. *Use of NSLs.* The *ODNI Transparency Report*, *supra*, reported that 12,150 NSLs were issued by the FBI in 2016, encompassing 24,801 requests for information.

[NSL p. 826, CTL p. 454. Insert after Note 4.]

D. THE TRUMP ADMINISTRATION
TRAVEL BANS[13]

In December 2015, then-presidential candidate Donald Trump published a statement on his campaign website proposing "a total and complete shutdown of Muslims entering the United States until our country's representatives can figure out what is going on." In tweets and media interviews he explained, "We're having problems with Muslims, and we're having problems with Muslims coming into the country," and "you have to deal with the mosques whether you like it or not." In an interview with CNN he added, "I think Islam hates us," and "[W]e can't allow people coming into the country who have this hatred."

When these and other statements drew criticism, he responded, "Calls to ban Muslims from entering the U.S. are offensive and unconstitutional. So you call it territories. OK? We're gonna do territories." He later added, "I'm looking now at territories. People were

---

13. At this writing, the Supreme Court has granted certiorari from *International Refugee Assistance Project v. Trump ("IRAP")*, 857 F.3d 554 (4th Cir. May 25, 2017) (en banc) — the Fourth Circuit decision which follows this introduction — and *Hawaii v. Trump*, 859 F.3d 741 (9th Cir. June 12, 2017) (per curiam). *See Trump v. IRAP*, 137 S. Ct. 2080 (2017) (per curiam). Realizing that new developments will very likely soon supersede the current materials, we have chosen to provide a short history of the travel bans through early July 2017, as well as excerpts from the two most recent appellate opinions analyzing the merits at that date, in the hope that the history will prove useful in any event.

The history is drawn from the opinions, as well as from Joanna Walters, Edward Helmore & Saeed Kamali, *US Airports on Frontline as Donald Trump's Travel Ban Causes Chaos and Protests*, The Guardian, Jan. 28, 2017; Dan Merica, *How Trump's Travel Ban Affects Green Card Holders and Dual Citizens*, CNN, Jan. 29, 2017, http://www.cnn.com/2017/01/29/politics/donald-trump-travel-ban-green-card-dual-citizens/index.html; Glenn Kessler, *The Number of People Affected by Trump's Travel Ban: About 90,000*, Wash. Post, Jan. 30, 2017; and Louis Jacobson, *Trump's Travel Ban Executive Order, Take 2*, Politifact, Mar. 6, 2017, http://www.politifact.com/truth-o-meter/article/2017/mar/06/trumps-travel-ban-executive-order-take-2/.

We use the term "Travel Ban" because the President has. *See* Eugene Scott, *Trump Criticizes Latest Court Ruling Against Travel Ban*, CNN, June 13, 2017, http://www.cnn.com/2017/06/13/politics/trump-tweet-ban-ninth-court/index.html.

so upset when I used the word Muslim. Oh, you can't use the word
Muslim. Remember this. I'm okay with that, because I'm talking
territory instead of Muslim."

Just a week after taking office, President Trump signed Executive
Order No. 13,769 ("EO-1"), which suspended travel for 90 days from
Iran, Libya, Somalia, Sudan, Syria, Yemen, and Iraq (all Muslim-
majority countries),[14] blocked the admittance of all Syrian refugees
indefinitely, and halted other refugee admissions for 120 days.[15] He said,
"This is the 'Protection of the Nation from Foreign Terrorist Entry into
the United States.' We all know what that means." The next day,
presidential advisor Rudolph Giuliani explained, "So when [the
President] first announced it, he said 'Muslim ban.' He called me up. He
said, 'Put a commission together. Show me the right way to do it
legally.'" Giuliani then said that he had assembled a group of lawyers
who "focused on, instead of religion, danger — the areas of the world
that create danger for us."

EO-1 went into effect immediately and applied to permanent U.S.
residents (green-card holders) as well as foreign visitors.[16] Confusion and
uncertainty surrounding the implementation of the order resulted in
hundreds being detained at airports or in transit, including lawful
permanent residents, students, work and tourist visa holders, and pre-
approved refugees.

Legal challenges to EO-1 were filed promptly. On the evening of
January 28, 2017, a federal judge issued an emergency stay on the
removal of individuals who had arrived in U.S. airports after the order
had been issued. *Darweesh v. Trump*, No. 1:17-cv-00480-AMD, 2017
WL 388504 (E.D.N.Y. Jan. 28, 2017). The order stopped the deportation
of travelers caught up in the ban and required the release of valid visa
holders being held at airports. The next day, a different federal judge
issued a temporary restraining order on the detention or removal of
individuals who had arrived legally from seven named countries.
Louhghalam v. Trump, No. 17-cv-10154, 2017 WL 386550 (D. Mass.
Jan. 29, 2017).

---

14. Iraq's population is 99% Muslim, Iran's is 99.5%, Libya's is 96.6%,
Sudan's is 90.7%, Somalia's is 99.8%, Syria's is 92.8%, and Yemen's is 99.1%.
See IRAP, 857 F.3d at 572 n.2 (citing Pew Res. Ctr., *The Global Religious
Landscape* 45-50 (2012)).

15. Exec. Order No. 13,769, 82 Fed. Reg. 8977 (Jan. 27, 2017).

16. The application of the order to lawful permanent residents was reversed
two days later under political pressure.

Multiple states, including Washington and Minnesota, filed a lawsuit in federal court alleging that they faced immediate and irreparable injury to their residents' employment, education, business, family relations, and freedom to travel. In a three-page opinion, the district court found that they had "raised at least serious questions going to the merits of their claims," and that they had met their burden of showing "significant and ongoing harm inflicted on [their residents] . . . ." *Washington v. Trump*, No. C17-0141JLR, 2017 WL 462040 (W.D. Wash. Feb. 3, 2017), *denial of emer. stay*, 847 F.3d 1151 (9th Cir.) (per curiam), *reh'g en banc denied*, 853 F.3d 933 (9th Cir.), *amended*, 858 F.3d 1168 (9th Cir. Mar. 17, 2017). On appeal, the Court of Appeals for the Ninth Circuit rejected the government's emergency request to lift the restraining order. 847 F.3d 1151. It then ruled that the government had provided no evidence of a terrorist threat posed by travelers from the countries in question, further stating that "[r]ather than present evidence to explain the need for the Executive Order, the Government has taken the position that we must not review its decision at all. We disagree . . . ." *Id.* at 1157. At the same time, it admitted:

> More generally, even if the TRO might be overbroad in some respects, it is not our role to try, in effect, to rewrite the Executive Order. The political branches are far better equipped to make appropriate distinctions. For now, it is enough for us to conclude that the Government has failed to establish that it will likely succeed on its due process argument in this appeal. [*Id.* at 1167.]

Heeding this invitation, the Administration rescinded EO-1 and published a superseding executive order with the same name, Executive Order No. 13,780 [EO-2], on March 6.

Executive Order No. 13,780,
Protecting the Nation from
Foreign Terrorist Entry into the United States
82 Fed. Reg. 13209 (Mar. 6, 2017)

By the authority vested in me as President by the Constitution and the laws of the United States of America, including the Immigration and Nationality Act (INA), 8 U.S.C. 1101 et seq., and section 301 of title 3, United States Code, and to protect the Nation from terrorist activities by

foreign nationals admitted to the United States, it is hereby ordered as
follows:

Sec. 1. Policy and Purpose.

(a) It is the policy of the United States to protect its citizens from
terrorist attacks, including those committed by foreign nationals. The
screening and vetting protocols and procedures associated with the visa-
issuance process and the United States Refugee Admissions Program
(USRAP) play a crucial role in detecting foreign nationals who may
commit, aid, or support acts of terrorism and in preventing those
individuals from entering the United States. It is therefore the policy
of the United States to improve the screening and vetting protocols
and procedures associated with the visa-issuance process and the
USRAP. . . .

(b) . . .

> (iv) [EO-1] did not provide a basis for discriminating for or
> against members of any particular religion. While that order
> allowed for prioritization of refugee claims from members of
> persecuted religious minority groups, that priority applied to
> refugees from every nation, including those in which Islam is a
> minority religion, and it applied to minority sects within a
> religion. That order was not motivated by animus toward any
> religion, but was instead intended to protect the ability of
> religious minorities — whoever they are and wherever they
> reside — to avail themselves of the USRAP in light of their
> particular challenges and circumstances. . . .

(d) Nationals from the countries previously identified under section
217(a)(12) of the INA warrant additional scrutiny in connection with our
immigration policies because the conditions in these countries present
heightened threats. Each of these countries is a state sponsor of terrorism,
has been significantly compromised by terrorist organizations, or
contains active conflict zones. Any of these circumstances diminishes the
foreign government's willingness or ability to share or validate important
information about individuals seeking to travel to the
United States. Moreover, the significant presence in each of these
countries of terrorist organizations, their members, and others exposed to
those organizations increases the chance that conditions will be exploited
to enable terrorist operatives or sympathizers to travel to the United
States. Finally, once foreign nationals from these countries are admitted
to the United States, it is often difficult to remove them, because many of

these countries typically delay issuing, or refuse to issue, travel documents. . . .

(f) In light of the conditions in . . . [Iran, Libya, Somalia, Sudan, Syria, and Yemen], until the assessment of current screening and vetting procedures required by section 2 of this order is completed, the risk of erroneously permitting entry of a national of one of these countries who intends to commit terrorist acts or otherwise harm the national security of the United States is unacceptably high. Accordingly, while that assessment is ongoing, I am imposing a temporary pause on the entry of nationals from Iran, Libya, Somalia, Sudan, Syria, and Yemen, subject to categorical exceptions and case-by-case waivers, as described in section 3 of this order. . . .

(h) Recent history shows that some of those who have entered the United States through our immigration system have proved to be threats to our national security. Since 2001, hundreds of persons born abroad have been convicted of terrorism-related crimes in the United States. They have included not just persons who came here legally on visas but also individuals who first entered the country as refugees. For example, in January 2013, two Iraqi nationals admitted to the United States as refugees in 2009 were sentenced to 40 years and to life in prison, respectively, for multiple terrorism-related offenses. And in October 2014, a native of Somalia who had been brought to the United States as a child refugee and later became a naturalized United States citizen was sentenced to 30 years in prison for attempting to use a weapon of mass destruction as part of a plot to detonate a bomb at a crowded Christmas-tree-lighting ceremony in Portland, Oregon. The Attorney General has reported to me that more than 300 persons who entered the United States as refugees are currently the subjects of counterterrorism investigations by the Federal Bureau of Investigation.

(i) Given the foregoing, the entry into the United States of foreign nationals who may commit, aid, or support acts of terrorism remains a matter of grave concern. In light of the Ninth Circuit's observation that the political branches are better suited to determine the appropriate scope of any suspensions than are the courts, and in order to avoid spending additional time pursuing litigation, I am revoking Executive Order 13769 and replacing it with this order, which expressly excludes from the suspensions categories of aliens that have prompted judicial concerns and which clarifies or refines the approach to certain other issues or categories of affected aliens.

Sec. 2.   Temporary Suspension of Entry for Nationals of Countries of Particular Concern During Review Period.

(a) The Secretary of Homeland Security, in consultation with the Secretary of State and the Director of National Intelligence, shall conduct a worldwide review to identify whether, and if so what, additional information will be needed from each foreign country to adjudicate an application by a national of that country for a visa, admission, or other benefit under the INA (adjudications) in order to determine that the individual is not a security or public-safety threat. . . .

(c) . . . [T]o ensure the proper review and maximum utilization of available resources for the screening and vetting of foreign nationals, to ensure that adequate standards are established to prevent infiltration by foreign terrorists, and in light of the national security concerns referenced in section 1 of this order, I hereby proclaim, pursuant to sections 212(f) and 215(a) of the INA, 8 U.S.C. 1182(f) and 1185(a), that the unrestricted entry into the United States of nationals of Iran, Libya, Somalia, Sudan, Syria, and Yemen would be detrimental to the interests of the United States. I therefore direct that the entry into the United States of nationals of those six countries be suspended for 90 days from the effective date of this order, subject to the limitations, waivers, and exceptions set forth in sections 3 and 12 of this order. . . .

Sec. 3. Scope and Implementation of Suspension.

(a) Scope. Subject to the exceptions set forth in subsection (b) of this section and any waiver under subsection (c) of this section, the suspension of entry pursuant to section 2 of this order shall apply only to foreign nationals of the designated countries who:

  (i) are outside the United States on the effective date of this order;

  (ii) did not have a valid visa at 5:00 p.m., eastern standard time on January 27, 2017; and

  (iii) do not have a valid visa on the effective date of this order.

(b) Exceptions. The suspension of entry pursuant to section 2 of this order shall not apply to:

  (i) any lawful permanent resident of the United States;

  (ii) . . . [various foreign nationals who are traveling with certain documentation or who have been granted asylum].

(c) Waivers. [The Commissioner of U.S. Customs and Border Protection is delegated the authority to waive the country restrictions on a case-by-case basis for hardship.] . . .

Sec. 6. Realignment of the U.S. Refugee Admissions Program for Fiscal Year 2017.

(a) The Secretary of State shall suspend travel of refugees into the United States under the USRAP, and the Secretary of Homeland Security shall suspend decisions on applications for refugee status, for 120 days after the effective date of this order, subject to waivers pursuant to subsection (c) of this section. During the 120-day period, the Secretary of State . . . shall review the USRAP application and adjudication processes to determine what additional procedures should be used to ensure that individuals seeking admission as refugees do not pose a threat to the security and welfare of the United States, and shall implement such additional procedures. The suspension described in this subsection shall not apply to refugee applicants who, before the effective date of this order, have been formally scheduled for transit by the Department of State. . . .

(b) Pursuant to section 212(f) of the INA, I hereby proclaim that the entry of more than 50,000 refugees in fiscal year 2017 would be detrimental to the interests of the United States, and thus suspend any entries in excess of that number until such time as I determine that additional entries would be in the national interest.

(c) Notwithstanding the temporary suspension imposed pursuant to subsection (a) of this section, the Secretary of State and the Secretary of Homeland Security may jointly determine to admit individuals to the United States as refugees on a case-by-case basis, in their discretion, but only so long as they determine that the entry of such individuals as refugees is in the national interest and does not pose a threat to the security or welfare of the United States, including in circumstances such as the following: the individual's entry would enable the United States to conform its conduct to a preexisting international agreement or arrangement, or the denial of entry would cause undue hardship. . . .

Donald J. Trump

Lawsuits were immediately filed challenging EO-2, asserting both statutory and constitutional (chiefly Establishment Clause) claims. In *IRAP v. Trump*, No. TDC-17-0361, 2017 WL 1018235 (D. Md. Mar. 16, 2017), *aff'd in part, vacated in part*, 857 F.3d 554 (4th Cir. May 25, 2017) (en banc), the parties relied partly on the Immigration and Nationality Act (INA). The government invoked the President's authority under INA §1182(f), while the plaintiffs argued that this authority was subject to INA §1152(a)(1)(A), the INA's anti-discrimination provision.

Immigration and Nationality Act
8 U.S.C. §1101 *et seq.* (2012)

§1152. Numerical Limitations on Individual Foreign States

(a) Per Country Level
    (1) Nondiscrimination
        (A) Except as specifically provided in paragraph (2) and in sections 1101(a)(27), 1151(b)(2)(A)(i), and 1153 of this title, no person shall receive any preference or priority or be discriminated against in the issuance of an immigrant visa because of the person's race, sex, nationality, place of birth, or place of residence. . . .

§1182(f). Inadmissible Aliens . . .

(f) Suspension of Entry or Imposition of Restrictions by President. Whenever the President finds that the entry of any aliens or of any class of aliens into the United States would be detrimental to the interests of the United States, he may by proclamation, and for such period as he shall deem necessary, suspend the entry of all aliens or any class of aliens as immigrants or nonimmigrants, or impose on the entry of aliens any restrictions he may deem to be appropriate. . . .

In the Maryland case,[17] the district court agreed with Plaintiffs, holding:

> Because there is no clear basis to conclude that [the President's authority under] §1182(f) is exempt from the non-discrimination provision of §1152(a) or that the President is authorized to impose nationality-based distinctions on the immigrant visa issuance process through another statutory provision, the Court concludes that Plaintiffs have shown a likelihood of success on the merits of their claim that the Second Executive Order violates §1152(a), but only as to the issuance of immigrant visas, which the statutory language makes clear is the extent of the scope of that anti-discrimination requirement. [*IRAP*, 2017 WL 1018235, at *10.]

It also held that the plaintiffs had established a likelihood of success on their Establishment Clause claim, finding that:

> while the travel ban bears no resemblance to any response to a national security risk in recent history, it bears a clear resemblance to the precise action that President Trump described as effectuating his Muslim ban. Thus, it is more likely that the primary purpose of the travel ban was grounded in religion, and even if the Second Executive Order has a national security purpose, it is likely that its primary purpose remains the effectuation of the proposed Muslim ban. [*Id.* at *16.]

The court then enjoined Section 2(c) of EO-2 (the ban on the entry of citizens from the six Muslim-majority countries) nationwide. On the government's appeal, the Court of Appeals for the Fourth Circuit, sitting en banc, affirmed the district court ruling in substantial part by a 10-3 vote. 857 F.3d 554. Excerpts of that opinion are presented *infra*. The Supreme Court has since granted the government's petition for certiorari and partially stayed the Fourth Circuit's ruling, as noted *infra*.

In *Hawai'i v. Trump,* No. 17-00050 DKW-KSC, 2017 WL 1011673 (D. Haw. Mar 15, 2017), *affirmed in part, vacated in part*, 859 F.3d 741 (9th Cir. June 12, 2017) (per curiam), the district court relied on

---

17. Additional district court rulings on EO-2 include *Washington v. Trump*, No. 2:17-cv-00141-JLR, 2017 WL 511013 (W.D. Wash. Jan. 30, 2017), and *Ali v. Trump*, No. 2:17-cv-00135-JLR (W.D. Wash. Jan 30, 2017), which were stayed pending a Ninth Circuit decision in *Hawai'i v. Trump*, 859 F.3d 741 (9th Cir. June 12, 2017) (per curiam); and *Al-Mowafek v. Trump*, No. 3:17-cv-00557 (N.D. Cal. Feb. 2, 2017), and *Sarsour v. Trump*, No. 1:17-cv-00120 AJT-IDD, 2017 WL 1113305 (E.D. Va. Mar. 24, 2017), which have been stayed pending the Supreme Court's review of *IRAP* and *Hawaii*.

statements by both candidate and President Trump and his advisers, in ruling for the Plaintiffs on their Establishment Clause claim.

> These plainly-worded statements, made in the months leading up to and contemporaneous with the signing of the Executive Order, and, in many cases, made by the Executive himself, betray the Executive Order's stated secular purpose. Any reasonable, objective observer would conclude, as does the Court for purposes of the instant Motion for TRO, that the stated secular purpose of the Executive Order is, at the very least, "secondary to a religious objective" of temporarily suspending the entry of Muslims. [2017 WL 1011673, at *14 (citation omitted).]

The court issued a nationwide temporary restraining order of EO-2's 120-day ban on the admission of refugees and its 90-day ban on immigrants from listed countries, which it subsequently converted to a preliminary injunction. On the government's appeal, the Court of Appeals for the Ninth Circuit affirmed on statutory grounds without reaching the constitutional claims, though it slightly narrowed the scope of the preliminary injunction to exclude purely internal review processes within the executive branch. 859 F.3d 741. An excerpt of its opinion follows *IRAP*.

International Refugee Assistance Project v. Trump
United States Court of Appeals, Fourth Circuit, May 25, 2017 (en banc)
857 F.3d 554
cert. granted and stay applications granted in part,
137 S. Ct. 2080 (U.S. June 26, 2017) (per curiam)

GREGORY, Chief Judge: The question for this Court, distilled to its essential form, is whether the Constitution, as the Supreme Court declared in *Ex parte Milligan*, 71 U.S. (4 Wall.) 2, 120 (1866), remains "a law for rulers and people, equally in war and in peace." And if so, whether it protects Plaintiffs' right to challenge an Executive Order that in text speaks with vague words of national security, but in context drips with religious intolerance, animus, and discrimination. Surely the Establishment Clause of the First Amendment yet stands as an untiring sentinel for the protection of one of our most cherished founding principles — that government shall not establish any religious orthodoxy, or favor or disfavor one religion over another. Congress granted the President broad power to deny entry to aliens, but that power is not absolute. It cannot go unchecked when, as here, the President wields it through an executive edict that stands to cause irreparable harm to individuals across this nation. Therefore, for the reasons that follow, we affirm in substantial part the district court's issuance of a nationwide preliminary injunction as to Section 2(c) of the challenged Executive Order.

I. . . .

C.

This action was brought by six individuals, all American citizens or lawful permanent residents who have at least one family member seeking entry into the United States from one of the Designated Countries, and three organizations that serve or represent Muslim clients or members. . .

D.

Plaintiffs initiated this suit on February 7, 2017, seeking declaratory and injunctive relief against enforcement of the First Executive Order. Plaintiffs claimed that EO-1 violated the Establishment Clause of the First Amendment; the equal protection component of the Due Process Clause of the Fifth Amendment; the Immigration and Nationality Act ("INA"), 8 U.S.C. §§1101-1537 (2012); the Religious Freedom Restoration Act, 42 U.S.C. §§2000bb to 2000bb-4 (2012); the Refugee Act, 8 U.S.C. §§1521-24 (2012); and the Administrative Procedure Act, 5 U.S.C. §§701-706 (2012). They named as Defendants the President, DHS, the Department of State, the Office of the Director of National Intelligence, the Secretary of Homeland Security, the Secretary of State, and the Director of National Intelligence. . . .

[The district court had issued a nationwide preliminary injunction against any enforcement of EO-2 §2(c) based on the plaintiffs' constitutional claim. The appeals court reasoned that even were it to conclude that EO-2 violated the INA (as the district court also ruled), it still had to reach the constitutional claim to decide the scope of the preliminary injunction. In light of this posture, it did not address the statutory question.]

III.

[The Court found that the constitutional challenge was justiciable (compare *Washington v. Trump*, 847 F.3d 1151 (9th Cir. 2017), p. 1 in this *Supplement, supra*), and that the plaintiffs had standing.] . . .

IV.

A preliminary injunction is an "extraordinary remed[y] involving the exercise of very far-reaching power" and is "to be granted only sparingly and in limited circumstances." *MicroStrategy Inc. v. Motorola, Inc.*, 245 F.3d 335, 339 (4th Cir. 2001) (quoting *Direx Israel, Ltd. v. Breakthrough Med. Corp.*, 952 F.2d 802, 816 (4th Cir. 1991)). For a district court to grant a preliminary injunction, "a plaintiff 'must establish [1] that he is likely to succeed on the merits, [2] that he is likely to suffer irreparable harm in the absence of preliminary relief, [3] that the balance of equities tips in his favor, and [4] that an injunction is in the public interest.'" *WV Ass'n of Club Owners & Fraternal Servs., Inc. v. Musgrave*, 553 F.3d 292, 298 (4th Cir. 2009) (quoting *Winter v. Nat. Res. Defense Council, Inc.*, 555 U.S. 7, 20 (2008)). The district court found that Plaintiffs satisfied all four requirements as to their Establishment Clause claim, and it enjoined Section 2(c) of EO-2. We evaluate the court's findings for abuse of discretion, reviewing its factual findings for clear error and its legal conclusions de novo.

A.

The district court determined that Plaintiffs are likely to succeed on the merits of their claim that EO-2 violates the Establishment Clause. It found that because EO-2 is "facially neutral in terms of religion," [*IRAP v. Trump,* No. TDC-17-0361, 2017 WL 1018235 (D. Md. Mar. 16, 2017)], at *13, the test outlined in *Lemon v. Kurtzman*, 403 U.S. 602 (1971), governs the constitutional inquiry. And applying the *Lemon* test, the court found that EO-2 likely violates the Establishment Clause. The Government argues that the court erroneously applied the *Lemon* test instead of the more deferential test set forth in *Kleindienst v. Mandel*, 408 U.S. 753 (1972). And under *Mandel*, the Government contends, Plaintiffs' claim fails.

1. . . . .

In *Mandel*, American university professors had invited Mandel, a
Belgian citizen and revolutionary Marxist and professional journalist, to
speak at a number of conferences in the United States. 408 U.S. at 756.
But Mandel's application for a nonimmigrant visa was denied under a
then-existing INA provision that barred the entry of aliens "who
advocate the economic, international, and governmental doctrines of
world communism." 8 U.S.C. §1182(a)(28)(D) (1964). The Attorney
General had discretion to waive §1182(a)(28)(D)'s bar and grant Mandel
an individual exception, but declined to do so on the grounds that
Mandel had violated the terms of his visas during prior visits to the
United States. 408 U.S. at 759. The American professors sued, alleging,
among other things, that the denial of Mandel's visa violated their First
Amendment rights to "hear his views and engage him in a free and open
academic exchange." *Id.* at 760.

The Supreme Court, citing "Congress' 'plenary power to make rules
for the admission of aliens and to exclude those who possess those
characteristics which Congress has forbidden,'" *id.* at 766 (quoting
Boutilier v. INS, 387 U.S. 118, 123 (1967)), found that the longstanding
principle of deference to the political branches in the immigration
context limited its review of plaintiffs' challenge, *id.* at 767. The Court
held that "when the Executive exercises this power [to exclude an alien]
on the basis of a facially legitimate and bona fide reason, the courts will
neither look behind the exercise of that discretion, nor test it by
balancing its justification against the [plaintiffs'] First Amendment
interests." *Id.* at 770. The Court concluded that the Attorney General's
stated reason for denying Mandel's visa — that he had violated the terms
of prior visas — satisfied this test. It therefore did not review plaintiffs'
First Amendment claim. . . .

But in another more recent line of cases, the Supreme Court has
made clear that despite the political branches' plenary power over
immigration, that power is still "subject to important constitutional
limitations," *Zadvydas v. Davis*, 533 U.S. 678, 695 (2001), and that it is
the judiciary's responsibility to uphold those limitations. [*Immigration &
Naturalization Service v. Chadha* , 462 U.S. 919, 941 (1983)] (stating
that Congress and the Executive must "cho[ose] a constitutionally
permissible means of implementing" their authority over immigration).
These cases instruct that the political branches' power over immigration
is not tantamount to a constitutional blank check, and that vigorous

judicial review is required when an immigration action's constitutionality is in question.

We are bound to give effect to both lines of cases, meaning that we must enforce constitutional limitations on immigration actions while also applying *Mandel*'s deferential test to those actions as the Supreme Court has instructed. For the reasons that follow, however, we find that these tasks are not mutually exclusive, and that *Mandel*'s test still contemplates meaningful judicial review of constitutional challenges in certain, narrow circumstances, as we have here.

To begin, *Mandel*'s test undoubtedly imposes a heavy burden on plaintiffs, consistent with the significant deference we afford the political branches in the immigration context. *See Mathews v. Diaz*, 426 U.S. 67, 82 (1976) (describing the "narrow standard of [judicial] review of decisions made by the Congress or the President in the area of immigration and naturalization"). The government need only show that the challenged action is "facially legitimate and bona fide" to defeat a constitutional challenge. *Mandel*, 408 U.S. at 770. These are separate and quite distinct requirements. To be "facially legitimate," there must be a valid reason for the challenged action stated on the face of the action. [*Kerry v. Din*], 135 S. Ct. 2128, 2140-41 (2015) (Kennedy, J., concurring in the judgment) (finding visa denial "facially legitimate" where government cited a statutory provision in support of the denial).

And as the name suggests, the "bona fide" requirement concerns whether the government issued the challenged action in good faith. In *Kerry v. Din*, Justice Kennedy, joined by Justice Alito, elaborated on this requirement. *Id.* at 2141. Here, the burden is on the plaintiff. Justice Kennedy explained that where a plaintiff makes "an affirmative showing of bad faith" that is "plausibly alleged with sufficient particularity," courts may "look behind" the challenged action to assess its "facially legitimate" justification. *Id.* (suggesting that if plaintiff had sufficiently alleged that government denied visa in bad faith, court should inquire whether the government's stated statutory basis for denying the visa was the actual reason for the denial). In the typical case, it will be difficult for a plaintiff to make an affirmative showing of bad faith with plausibility and particularity. And absent this affirmative showing, courts must defer to the government's "facially legitimate" reason for the action.

Mandel therefore clearly sets a high bar for plaintiffs seeking judicial review of a constitutional challenge to an immigration action. But although *Mandel*'s "facially legitimate and bona fide" test affords significant deference to the political branches' decisions in this area, it does not completely insulate those decisions from *any* meaningful review. Where plaintiffs have seriously called into question whether the stated reason for the challenged action was provided in good faith, we understand *Mandel*, as construed by Justice Kennedy in his controlling concurrence in *Din*, to require that we step away from our deferential posture and look behind the stated reason for the challenged action. In other words, *Mandel*'s requirement that an immigration action be "bona fide" may in some instances compel more searching judicial review. Plaintiffs ask this Court to engage in such searching review here under the traditional Establishment Clause test, and we therefore turn to consider whether such a test is warranted.

We start with *Mandel*'s requirement that the challenged government action be "facially legitimate." EO-2's stated purpose is "to protect the Nation from terrorist activities by foreign nationals admitted to the United States." EO-2, Preamble. We find that this stated national security interest is, on its face, a valid reason for Section 2(c)'s suspension of entry. EO-2 therefore satisfies *Mandel*'s first requirement. Absent allegations of bad faith, our analysis would end here in favor of the Government. But in this case, Plaintiffs have alleged that EO-2's stated purpose was given in bad faith. We therefore must consider whether they have made the requisite showing of bad faith.

As noted, Plaintiffs must "plausibly allege[ ] with sufficient particularity" that the reason for the government action was provided in bad faith. *Din*, 135 S. Ct. at 2141 (Kennedy, J., concurring in the judgment). Plaintiffs here claim that EO-2 invokes national security in bad faith, as a pretext for what really is an anti-Muslim religious purpose. Plaintiffs point to ample evidence that national security is not the true reason for EO-2, including, among other things, then-candidate Trump's numerous campaign statements expressing animus towards the Islamic faith; his proposal to ban Muslims from entering the United States; his subsequent explanation that he would effectuate this ban by targeting "territories" instead of Muslims directly; the issuance of EO-1, which targeted certain majority-Muslim nations and included a preference for religious minorities; an advisor's statement that the President had asked him to find a way to ban Muslims in a legal way; and the issuance of EO-2, which resembles EO-1 and which President Trump and his advisors described as having the same policy goals as EO-1. Plaintiffs also point to the comparably weak evidence that EO-2 is meant to address national security interests, including the exclusion of national security agencies from the decisionmaking process, the post hoc nature of the national security rationale, and evidence from DHS that EO-2 would not operate to diminish the threat of potential terrorist activity.

Based on this evidence, we find that Plaintiffs have more than plausibly alleged that EO-2's stated national security interest was provided in bad faith, as a pretext for its religious purpose. And having concluded that the "facially legitimate" reason proffered by the government is not "bona fide," we no longer defer to that reason and instead may "look behind" EO-2. *Din*, 135 S. Ct. at 2141 (Kennedy, J., concurring in the judgment). . . .

2.

To prevail under the *Lemon* test, the Government must show that the challenged action (1) "ha[s] a secular legislative purpose," (2) that "its principal or primary effect [is] one that neither advances nor inhibits religion," and (3) that it does "not foster 'an excessive government entanglement with religion.'" *Lemon*, 403 U.S. at 612-13 (quoting *Walz v. Tax Comm'n of the City of New York*, 397 U.S. 664, 674 (1970)) (citation omitted). The Government must satisfy all three prongs of *Lemon* to defeat an Establishment Clause challenge. *Edwards v. Aguillard*, 482 U.S. 578, 583 (1987). The dispute here centers on *Lemon*'s first prong.

In the Establishment Clause context, "purpose matters." *McCreary [County v. ACLU of Ky.*, 545 U.S. 844,] at 866 n.14. Under the *Lemon* test's first prong, the Government must show that the challenged action "ha[s] a secular legislative purpose." *Lemon*, 403 U.S. at 612. Accordingly, the Government must show that the challenged action has a secular purpose that is "genuine, not a sham, and not merely secondary to a religious objective." *McCreary*, 545 U.S. at 864; *see also Santa Fe Indep. Sch. Dist. v. Doe*, 530 U.S. 290, 308 (2000) ("When a governmental entity professes a secular purpose for an arguably religious policy, the government's characterization is, of course, entitled to some deference. But it is nonetheless the duty of the courts to 'distinguis[h] a sham secular purpose from a sincere one.'" (quoting *Wallace*, 472 U.S. at 75 (O'Connor, J., concurring in the judgment))). The government cannot meet this requirement by identifying *any* secular purpose for the challenged action. *McCreary*, 545 U.S. at 865 n.13 (noting that if any secular purpose sufficed, "it would leave the purpose test with no real bite, given the ease of finding some secular purpose for almost any government action"). Rather, the government must show that the challenged action's *primary* purpose is secular. *Edwards*, 482 U.S. at 594 (finding an Establishment Clause violation where the challenged act's "primary purpose . . . is to endorse a particular religious doctrine," notwithstanding that the act's stated purpose was secular).

When a court considers whether a challenged government action's primary purpose is secular, it attempts to discern the "official objective . . . from readily discoverable fact, without any judicial psychoanalysis of a drafter's heart of hearts." *McCreary*, 545 U.S. at 862. The court acts as a reasonable, "objective observer," taking into account "the traditional external signs that show up in the 'text, legislative history, and implementation of the statute,' or comparable official act." *Id.* (quoting *Santa Fe*, 530 U.S. at 308). It also considers the action's "historical context" and "the specific sequence of events leading to [its] passage." *Edwards*, 482 U.S. at 595. And as a reasonable observer, a court has a "reasonable memor[y]," and it cannot "'turn a blind eye to the context in which [the action] arose.'" *McCreary*, 545 U.S. at 866 (quoting *Santa Fe*, 530 U.S. at 315).

The evidence in the record, viewed from the standpoint of the reasonable observer, creates a compelling case that EO-2's primary purpose is religious. Then-candidate Trump's campaign statements reveal that on numerous occasions, he expressed anti-Muslim sentiment, as well as his intent, if elected, to ban Muslims from the United States. For instance, on December 7, 2015, Trump posted on his campaign website a "Statement on Preventing Muslim Immigration," in which he "call[ed] for a total and complete shutdown of Muslims entering the United States until our representatives can figure out what is going on" and remarked, "[I]t is obvious to anybody that the hatred is beyond comprehension. . . . [O]ur country cannot be the victims of horrendous attacks by people that believe only in Jihad, and have no sense of reason or respect for human life." In a March 9, 2016 interview, Trump stated that "Islam hates us," and that "[w]e can't allow people coming into this country who have this hatred." Less than two weeks later, in a March 22 interview, Trump again called for excluding Muslims, because "we're having problems with the Muslims, and we're having problems with Muslims coming into the country." And on December 21, 2016, when asked whether recent attacks in Europe affected his proposed Muslim ban, President-Elect Trump replied, "You know my plans. All along, I've proven to be right. 100% correct."

As a candidate, Trump also suggested that he would attempt to circumvent scrutiny of the Muslim ban by formulating it in terms of nationality, rather than religion. On July 17, 2016, in response to a tweet stating, "Calls to ban Muslims from entering the U.S. are offensive and unconstitutional," Trump said, "So you call it territories. OK? We're gonna do territories." One week later, Trump asserted that entry should be "immediately suspended [ed] . . . from any nation that has been compromised by terrorism." When asked whether this meant he was "roll[ing] back" his call for a Muslim ban, he said his plan was an "expansion" and explained that "[p]eople were so upset when I used the word Muslim," so he was instead "talking territory instead of Muslim."

Significantly, the First Executive Order appeared to take this exact form, barring citizens of seven predominantly Muslim countries from entering the United States. And just before President Trump signed EO-1 on January 27, 2017, he stated, "This is the 'Protection of the Nation from Foreign Terrorist Entry into the United States.' We all know what that means." The next day, presidential advisor and former New York City Mayor Giuliani appeared on Fox News and asserted that "when [Trump] first announced it, he said, 'Muslim ban.' He called me up. He said, 'Put a commission together. Show me the right way to do it legally.'"

Shortly after courts enjoined the First Executive Order, President Trump issued EO-2, which the President and members of his team characterized as being substantially similar to EO-1. EO-2 has the same name and basic structure as EO-1, but it does not include a preference for religious-minority refugees and excludes Iraq from its list of Designated Countries. EO-2, §1(e). It also exempts certain categories of nationals from the Designated Countries and institutes a waiver process for qualifying individuals. EO-2, §3(b), (c). Senior Policy Advisor [Stephen] Miller described the changes to EO-2 as "mostly minor technical differences," and said that there would be "the same basic policy outcomes for the country." White House Press Secretary [Sean] Spicer stated that "[t]he principles of the [second] executive order remain the same." And President Trump, in a speech at a rally, described EO-2 as "a watered down version of the first order." These statements suggest that like EO-1, EO-2's purpose is to effectuate the promised Muslim ban, and that its changes from EO-1 reflect an effort to help it survive judicial scrutiny, rather than to avoid targeting Muslims for exclusion from the United States.

These statements, taken together, provide direct, specific evidence of what motivated both EO-1 and EO-2: President Trump's desire to exclude Muslims from the United States. The statements also reveal President Trump's intended means of effectuating the ban: by targeting majority-Muslim nations instead of Muslims explicitly. And after courts enjoined EO-1, the statements show how President Trump attempted to preserve its core mission: by issuing EO-2 — a "watered down" version with "the same basic policy outcomes." These statements are the exact

type of "readily discoverable fact[s]" that we use in determining a
government action's primary purpose. *McCreary*, 545 U.S. at 862. They
are explicit statements of purpose and are attributable either to President
Trump directly or to his advisors. We need not probe anyone's heart of
hearts to discover the purpose of EO-2, for President Trump and his
aides have explained it on numerous occasions and in no uncertain terms.
See Glassroth v. Moore, 335 F.3d 1282, 1296 (11th Cir. 2003) ("Besides,
no psychoanalysis or dissection is required here, where there is abundant
evidence, including his own words, of the [government actor's]
purpose."). EO-2 cannot be read in isolation from the statements of
planning and purpose that accompanied it, particularly in light of the
sheer number of statements, their nearly singular source, and the close
connection they draw between the proposed Muslim ban and EO-2 itself.
See McCreary, 545 U.S. at 866 (rejecting notion that court could
consider only "the latest news about the last in a series of
governmental actions, however close they may all be in time and
subject"). The reasonable observer could easily connect these statements
to EO-2 and understand that its primary purpose appears to be religious,
rather than secular.

The Government argues, without meaningfully addressing Plaintiffs'
proffered evidence, that EO-2's primary purpose is in fact secular
because it is facially neutral and operates to address the risks of potential
terrorism without targeting any particular religious group. That EO-2's
stated objective is religiously neutral is not dispositive; the entire premise
of our review under *Lemon* is that even facially neutral government
actions can violate the Establishment Clause. *See Lemon*, 403 U.S. at 612
(recognizing that "a law 'respecting' . . . . the establishment of religion[ ]
is not always easily identifiable as one," and creating a three-part test for
discerning when a facially neutral law violates the Establishment
Clause); *see also Santa Fe*, 530 U.S. at 315 ("Our examination [under
Lemon's purpose prong] . . . need not stop at an analysis of the text of the
policy."). We therefore reject the Government's suggestion that EO-2's
facial neutrality might somehow fully answer the question of EO-2's
primary purpose.

The Government's argument that EO-2's primary purpose is related
to national security is belied by evidence in the record that President
Trump issued the First Executive Order without consulting the relevant
national security agencies, and that those agencies only offered a national
security rationale after EO-1 was enjoined. Furthermore, internal reports
from DHS contradict this national security rationale, with one report
stating that "most foreign-born, US-based violent extremists likely

radicalized several years after their entry to the United States, limiting the ability of screening and vetting officials to prevent their entry because of national security concerns." According to former National Security Officials, Section 2(c) serves "no legitimate national security purpose," given that "not a single American has died in a terrorist attack on U.S. soil at the hands of citizens of these six nations in the last forty years" and that there is no evidence of any new security risks emanating from these countries. Corrected Brief for Former National Security Officials as Amici Curiae Supporting Appellees 5-8, ECF No. 126-1. Like the district court, we think this strong evidence that any national security justification for EO-2 was secondary to its primary religious purpose and was offered as more of a "litigating position" than as the actual purpose of EO-2. *See McCreary*, 545 U.S. at 871 (describing the government's "new statements of purpose . . . as a litigating position" where they were offered to explain the third iteration of a previously enjoined religious display). And EO-2's text does little to bolster any national security rationale: the only examples it provides of immigrants born abroad and convicted of terrorism-related crimes in the United States include two Iraqis — Iraq is not a designated country in EO-2 — and a Somalian refugee who entered the United States as a child and was radicalized here as an adult. EO-2, §1(h). The Government's asserted national security purpose is therefore no more convincing as applied to EO-2 than it was to EO-1.

Relatedly, the Government argues that EO-2's operation "confirms its stated purpose." "[I]t applies to six countries based on risk, not religion; and in those six countries, the suspension applies irrespective of any alien's religion." *Id.* In support of its argument that EO-2 does not single out Muslims, the Government notes that these six countries are either places where ISIS has a heavy presence (Syria), state sponsors of terrorism (Iran, Sudan, and Syria), or safe havens for terrorists (Libya, Somalia, and Yemen). The Government also points out that the six Designated Countries represent only a small proportion of the world's majority-Muslim nations, and EO-2 applies to everyone in those countries, even non-Muslims. This shows, the Government argues, that EO-2's primary purpose is secular. The trouble with this argument is that EO-2's practical operation is not severable from the myriad statements explaining its operation as intended to bar Muslims from the United States. And that EO-2 is underinclusive by targeting only a small percentage of the world's majority-Muslim nations and overinclusive for targeting all citizens, even non-Muslims, in the Designated Countries, is not responsive to the purpose inquiry. This evidence might be relevant to our analysis under *Lemon*'s second prong, which asks whether a government act has the primary *effect* of endorsing or disapproving of religion, *see Lynch v. Donnelly*, 465 U.S. 668, 692 (1984) (O'Connor, J., concurring), but it does not answer whether the government acted with a primarily religious purpose to begin with. If we limited our purpose inquiry to review of the operation of a facially neutral order, we would be caught in an analytical loop, where the order would always survive scrutiny. It is for this precise reason that when we attempt to discern purpose, we look to more than just the challenged action itself. And here, when we consider the full context of EO-2, it is evident that it is likely motivated primarily by religion. We do not discount that there may be a national security concern motivating EO-2; we merely find it likely that any such purpose is secondary to EO-2's religious purpose.

The Government separately contends that our purpose inquiry should not extend to "extrinsic evidence" that is beyond EO-2's relevant context. The Government first argues that we should not look beyond EO-2's "text and operation." But this is clearly incorrect, as the Supreme Court has explicitly stated that we review more than just the face of a challenged action. *See, e.g., Bd. of Educ. of Kiryas Joel Vill. Sch. Dist. v. Grumet*, 512 U.S. 687, 699 (1994) ("[O]ur [Establishment Clause] analysis does not end with the text of the statute at issue.") (citing *Church of the Lukumi Babalu Aye*, 508 U.S. at 534).[19]

---

19. The Government separately suggests that we should limit our review to EO-2's text and operation based on "the Constitution's structure and its separation of powers," and the "'presumption of regularity' that attaches to all federal officials' actions." In support of this point, the Government relies on pre-*McCreary* cases discussing, variously, judicial deference to an executive official's decision to deport an alien who had violated the terms of his admission to the United States, *Reno v. Am.-Arab Anti-Discrimination Comm.*, 525 U.S. 471, 491 (1999), the President's absolute immunity from damages liability based on his or her official acts, *Nixon v. Fitzgerald*, 457 U.S. 731, 749 (1982), and the presumptive privilege we afford a President's conversations and correspondence, *United States v. Nixon*, 418 U.S. 683, 708 (1974). These cases suggest that in certain circumstances, we insulate the President and other executive officials from judicial scrutiny in order to protect and promote the effective functioning of the executive branch. But these cases do not circumscribe our review of Establishment Clause challenges or hold that when a President's official acts violate the Constitution, the acts themselves are immune from judicial review. We find no support in this line of cases for the Government's argument that our review of EO-2's context is so limited. In fact, the Supreme Court has suggested quite the opposite. *See Zadvydas*, 533 U.S. at 695 ("Executive and Legislative Branch decisionmaking . . . power is subject to important constitutional

The Government next argues that even if we do look beyond EO-2 itself, under *McCreary*, we are limited to considering only "the operative terms of governmental action and official pronouncements," which we understand to mean only EO-2 itself and a letter signed by the Attorney General and the Secretary of State that largely echoes EO-2's text. We find no support for this view in *McCreary*. The *McCreary* Court considered "the traditional external signs that show up in the 'text, legislative history, and implementation of the [challenged action],'" 545 U.S. at 862 (quoting *Santa Fe*, 530 U.S. at 308), but it did not limit other courts' review to those particular terms. *Id.* Nor did it make such an artificial distinction between "official" and "unofficial" context. Rather, it relied on principles of "common sense" and the "reasonable observer[']s . . . reasonable memor[y]" to cull the relevant context surrounding the challenged action. *Id.* at 866. The Government would have us abandon this approach in favor of an unworkable standard that is contrary to the well-established framework for considering the context of a challenged government action.

And finally, the Government argues that even if we could consider unofficial acts and statements, we should not rely on campaign statements. Those statements predate President Trump's constitutionally significant "transition from private life to the Nation's highest public office," and as such, they are less probative than official statements, the Government contends. We recognize that in many cases, campaign statements may not reveal all that much about a government actor's purpose. But we decline to impose a bright-line rule against considering campaign statements, because as with any evidence, we must make an individualized determination as to a statement's relevancy and probative value in light of all the circumstances. The campaign statements here are probative of purpose because they are closely related in time, attributable to the primary decisionmaker, and specific and easily connected to the challenged action. *See Glassroth* [*v. Moore*, 335 F.3d 1282 (11th Cir. 2003)], at 1297 (reviewing an elected judge's campaign materials that proclaimed him the "Ten Commandment's Judge" as part of its inquiry into the constitutionality of a Ten Commandments display he installed); *see also Washington v. Seattle Sch. Dist. No. 1*, 458 U.S. 457, 463 (1982) (considering facially neutral campaign statements related to bussing in an equal protection challenge); *California v. United States*, 438 U.S. 645, 663-64 (1978) (referring to candidates' political platforms when considering the Reclamation Act of 1902); *Village of Arlington Heights*

---

limitations." (citing *Chadha*, 462 U.S. at 941-42)).

v. Metro. Hous. Dev. Corp., 429 U.S. 252, 266-68 (1977) (explaining
that in the equal protection context, "[w]hen there is [ ] proof that a
discriminatory purpose has been a motivating factor in the decision," a
court may consider "contemporary statements by members of the
decisionmaking body").

Just as the reasonable observer's "world is not made brand new
every morning," *McCreary*, 545 U.S. at 866, nor are we able to awake
without the vivid memory of these statements. We cannot shut our eyes
to such evidence when it stares us in the face, for "there's none so blind
as they that won't see." Jonathan Swift, *Polite Conversation* 174
(Chiswick Press ed., 1892). If and when future courts are confronted with
campaign or other statements proffered as evidence of governmental
purpose, those courts must similarly determine, on a case-by-case basis,
whether such statements are probative evidence of governmental
purpose. Our holding today neither limits nor expands their review.

The Government argues that reviewing campaign statements here
would encourage scrutiny of all religious statements ever made by
elected officials, even remarks from before they assumed office. But our
review creates no such sweeping implications, because as the Supreme
Court has counseled, our purpose analysis "demands a sensitive inquiry
into such circumstantial and direct evidence of intent as may be
available." *Village of Arlington Heights*, 429 U.S. at 266; *see also Lee v.
Weisman*, 505 U.S. 577, 597 (1992) ("Our Establishment Clause
jurisprudence remains a delicate and fact-sensitive one. . . ."). Just as a
reasonable observer would not understand general statements of religious
conviction to inform later government action, nor would we look to such
statements as evidence of purpose. A person's particular religious beliefs,
her college essay on religious freedom, a speech she gave on the Free
Exercise Clause — rarely, if ever, will such evidence reveal anything
about that person's actions once in office. For a past statement to be
relevant to the government's purpose, there must be a substantial,
specific connection between it and the challenged government action.
And here, in this highly unique set of circumstances, there is a direct link
between the President's numerous campaign statements promising a
Muslim ban that targets territories, the discrete action he took only one
week into office executing that exact plan, and EO-2, the "watered
down" version of that plan that "get[s] just about everything," and "in
some ways, more."

For similar reasons, we reject the Government's argument that our
review of these campaign statements will "inevitably 'chill political
debate during campaigns.'" (quoting *Phelps v. Hamilton*, 59 F.3d 1058,

1068 (10th Cir. 1995)). Not all — not even most — political debate will
have any relevance to a challenged government action. Indeed, this case
is unique not because we are considering campaign statements, but
because we have such directly relevant and probative statements of
government purpose at all. *See Smith v. Town of Clarkton*, 682 F.2d
1055, 1064 (4th Cir. 1982) (observing that government actors "seldom, if
ever, announce on the record that they are pursuing a particular course of
action because of their desire to discriminate"). To the extent that our
review chills campaign promises to condemn and exclude entire religious
groups, we think that a welcome restraint.

Lastly, the Government contends that we are ill-equipped to
"attempt[ ] to assess what campaign statements reveal about the
motivation for later action." The Government argues that to do so would
"mire [us] in a swamp of unworkable litigation," *id.* (quoting Amended
Order, *Washington v. Trump*, No. 17-35105, slip op. at 13 (9th Cir. Mar.
17, 2017) (Kozinski, J., dissenting from denial of reconsideration en
banc)), and "forc[e us] to wrestle with intractable questions," such as
"the level of generality at which a statement must be made, by whom,
and how long after its utterance the statement remains probative." *Id.* But
discerning the motives behind a challenged government action is a well-
established part of our purpose inquiry. *McCreary*, 545 U.S. at 861
("Examination of purpose is a staple of statutory interpretation that
makes up the daily fare of every appellate court in the country, and
governmental purpose is a key element of a good deal of constitutional
doctrine." (citations omitted)). . . . We therefore see nothing "intractable"
about evaluating a statement's probative value based on the identity of
the speaker and how specifically the statement relates to the challenged
government action, for this is surely a routine part of constitutional
analysis. And this analysis is even more straightforward here, because we
are not attempting to discern motive from many legislators' statements,
as in *Brown*, but rather are looking primarily to one person's statements
to discern that person's motive for taking a particular action once in
office. . . .

EO-2 cannot be divorced from the cohesive narrative linking it to the
animus that inspired it. In light of this, we find that the reasonable
observer would likely conclude that EO-2's primary purpose is to
exclude persons from the United States on the basis of their religious
beliefs. We therefore find that EO-2 likely fails *Lemon*'s purpose prong

in violation of the Establishment Clause.[22] Accordingly, we hold that the district court did not err in concluding that Plaintiffs are likely to succeed on the merits of their Establishment Clause claim. . . .

C. . . .

At the outset, we reject the notion that the President, because he or she represents the entire nation, suffers irreparable harm whenever an executive action is enjoined. This Court has held that the Government is "in no way harmed by issuance of a preliminary injunction which prevents [it] from enforcing restrictions likely to be found unconstitutional." *Centro Tepeyac*, 722 F.3d at 191 (quoting *Giovani Carandola, Ltd. v. Bason*, 303 F.3d 507, 521 (4th Cir. 2002)). "If anything," we said, "the system is improved by such an injunction."*Id.* (quoting *Giovani Carandola*, 303 F.3d at 521). Because Section 2(c) of EO-2 is likely unconstitutional, allowing it to take effect would therefore inflict the greater institutional injury. And we are not persuaded that the general deference we afford the political branches ought to nevertheless tip the equities in the Government's favor, for even the President's actions are not above judicial scrutiny, and especially not where those actions are likely unconstitutional. *See Zadvydas*, 533 U.S. at 695; *Chadha*, 462 U.S. at 941-42.

We are likewise unmoved by the Government's rote invocation of harm to "national security interests" as the silver bullet that defeats all other asserted injuries. *See United States v. Robel*, 389 U.S. 258, 264 (1967) ("Th[e] concept of 'national defense' cannot be deemed an end in itself, justifying any exercise of legislative power designed to promote

---

22. What is more, we think EO-2 would likely fail any purpose test, for whether religious animus motivates a government action is a fundamental part of our Establishment Clause inquiry no matter the degree of scrutiny that applies. *See, e.g., Town of Greece v. Galloway*, —— U.S. ——, 134 S. Ct. 1811, 1826 (2014) (upholding town's legislative prayer policy in part because "[i]n no instance did town leaders signal disfavor toward nonparticipants or suggest that their stature in the community was in any way diminished"); *Hernandez v. Comm'r of Internal Revenue*, 490 U.S. 680, 696 (1989) (finding that the challenged statute satisfied *Lemon*'s purpose prong in part because "there is no allegation that [it] was born of animus"); *Lynch*, 465 U.S. at 673 (stating that the Establishment Clause "forbids hostility toward any [religion]"); *see also* Brief for Constitutional Law Scholars 6-11. There is simply too much evidence that EO-2 was motivated by religious animus for it to survive any measure of constitutional review.

such a goal. Implicit in the term 'national defense' is the notion of defending those values and ideals which set this Nation apart. . . . [O]ur country has taken singular pride in the democratic ideals enshrined in its Constitution, and the most cherished of those ideals have found expression in the First Amendment. It would indeed be ironic if, in the name of national defense, we would sanction the subversion of one of those liberties . . . which makes the defense of the Nation worthwhile."). National security may be the most compelling of government interests, but this does not mean it will always tip the balance of the equities in favor of the government. *See Holder v. Humanitarian Law Project*, 561 U.S. 1, 34 (2010) (agreeing with the dissent that the government's "authority and expertise in [national security and foreign relations] matters do not automatically trump the Court's own obligation to secure the protection that the Constitution grants to individuals" (quoting *id.* at 61 (Breyer, J., dissenting))). A claim of harm to national security must still outweigh the competing claim of injury. Here and elsewhere, the Government would have us end our inquiry without scrutinizing either Section 2(c)'s stated purpose or the Government's asserted interests, but "unconditional deference to a government agent's invocation of 'emergency' . . . has a lamentable place in our history," *Patrolmen's Benevolent Ass'n of New York v. City of New York*, 310 F.3d 43, 53-54 (2d. Cir. 2002) (citing *Korematsu v. United States*, 323 U.S. 214, 223 (1944)), and is incompatible with our duty to evaluate the evidence before us.

As we previously determined, the Government's asserted national security interest in enforcing Section 2(c) appears to be a post hoc, secondary justification for an executive action rooted in religious animus and intended to bar Muslims from this country. We remain unconvinced that Section 2(c) has more to do with national security than it does with effectuating the President's promised Muslim ban. We do not discount that EO-2 may have some national security purpose, nor do we disclaim that the injunction may have some impact on the Government. But our inquiry, whether for determining Section 2(c)'s primary purpose or for weighing the harm to the parties, is one of balance, and on balance, we cannot say that the Government's asserted national security interest outweighs the competing harm to Plaintiffs of the likely Establishment Clause violation. . . .

When the government chooses sides on religious issues, the "inevitable result" is "hatred, disrespect and even contempt" towards those who fall on the wrong side of the line. *Engel v. Vitale*, 370 U.S. 421, 431 (1962). Improper government involvement with religion "tends to destroy government and to degrade religion," *id.*, encourage persecution of religious minorities and nonbelievers, and foster hostility and division in our pluralistic society. The risk of these harms is particularly acute here, where from the highest elected office in the nation has come an Executive Order steeped in animus and directed at a single religious group. "The fullest realization of true religious liberty requires that government neither engage in nor compel religious practices, that it effect no favoritism among sects or between religion and nonreligion, and that it work deterrence of no religious belief." *Sch. Dist. of Abington Twp. v. Schempp*, 374 U.S. 203, 305 (1963) (Goldberg, J. concurring). We therefore conclude that enjoining Section 2(c) promotes the public interest of the highest order. And because Plaintiffs have satisfied all the requirements for securing a preliminary injunction, we find that the district court did not abuse its discretion in enjoining Section 2(c) of EO-2.

V

[The Court found that the district court did not abuse its discretion in issuing a nationwide injunction.] . . .

Finally, the Government argues that the district court erred by issuing the injunction against the President himself. We recognize that "in general, 'this court has no jurisdiction of a bill to enjoin the President in the performance of his official duties,'" *Franklin v. Massachusetts*, 505 U.S. 788, 802-03 (1992) (opinion of O'Connor, J.) (quoting *Johnson*, 71 U.S. at 501), and that a "grant of injunctive relief against the President himself is extraordinary, and should . . . raise[ ] judicial eyebrows," *id.* at 802. In light of the Supreme Court's clear warning that such relief should be ordered only in the rarest of circumstances we find that the district court erred in issuing an injunction against the President himself. We therefore lift the injunction as to the President only. The court's preliminary injunction shall otherwise remain fully intact.

To be clear, our conclusion does not "in any way suggest[ ] that Presidential action is *unreviewable*. Review of the legality of Presidential action can ordinarily be obtained in a suit seeking to enjoin the officers who attempt to enforce the President's directive." *Franklin*, 505 U.S. at 828 (Scalia, J., concurring in part and concurring in the judgment). Even though the President is not "directly bound" by the injunction, we "assume it is substantially likely that the President . . . would abide by an authoritative interpretation" of Section 2(c) of the Second Executive Order. *Id.* at 803 (opinion of O'Connor, J.).

VI

For all of these reasons, we affirm in part and vacate in part the preliminary injunction awarded by the district court. We also deny as moot Defendants' motion for a stay pending appeal.

Affirmed in part, vacated in part.

[Opinion of TRAXLER, J., concurring in the judgment, is omitted.]

[Opinion of KEENAN, J., with whom THACKER, J., joins except as to Part II.A.i., concurring in part and concurring in the judgement, is omitted.]

WYNN, Circuit Judge, concurring: . . . I write separately because I believe Plaintiffs' claim that Section 2I exceeds the President's authority under the Immigration Act also is likely to succeed on the merits. That statute authorizes the President to suspend the "entry of any aliens or of any class of aliens" that he finds "would be detrimental to the interests of the United States." 8 U.S.C. §1182(f). Because the Executive Order here relies on national origin as a proxy for discrimination based on religious animus, the Government's argument that Section 2I's suspension on entry "falls squarely within the President's broad authority" under Section 1182(f) essentially contends that Congress delegated to the President virtually unfettered discretion to deny entry to any class of aliens, including to deny entry solely on the basis of nationality and religion. Not so. . . .

I

. . . In sum, the language of Section 1182(f), related provisions in the Immigration Act, and the "object and policy" of the statute do not "explicitly" state, much less provide a "clear indication," that Congress intended to delegate to the President wholly unconstrained authority to deny entry to any class of aliens, including based on invidiously discriminatory reasons. *See Zadvydas*, 533 U.S. at 697. Accordingly, Section 2(c) — which this Court finds was likely borne of the President's animus against Muslims and his intent to rely on national origin as a proxy to give effect to that animus — exceeds the authority Congress conferred on the President in Section 1182(f). As Judge Friendly put it, "Congress could not have intended to make relevant" to the President's exercise of his delegated authority to suspend the entry of aliens "invidious discrimination against a particular race or group." *Wong Wing Hang* [v. *I.N.S.*, 360 F.2d 715 (2d Cir. 1966),] at 719 (internal quotation marks omitted).

II . . .

One might argue, as President Trump seemed to suggest during the campaign, that *as a matter of statistical fact*, Muslims, and therefore nationals of the six predominantly Muslim countries covered by the Executive Order, disproportionately engage in acts of terrorism, giving rise to a *factual* inference that admitting such individuals would be detrimental to the interests of the United States. Indeed, viewing the Executive Order in its most favorable light, that is the precisely the rationale underlying Section 2(c). Setting aside the question of whether that *factual finding* is true, or even reasonable — which is, at best, highly debatable given the 180 million people in the countries subject to the suspension on entry and the 1.6 million Muslims worldwide — that is precisely the inference that the Framers of the Constitution and the Reconstruction Amendments concluded was impermissible as a matter of *constitutional law. Korematsu*, 323 U.S. at 240 (Murphy, J., dissenting). In particular, classifying individuals based solely on their race, nationality, or religion — and then relying on those classifications to discriminate against certain races, nationalities, or religions — necessarily results in placing special burdens on individuals who lack any moral responsibility, a result the Framers deemed antithetical to core democratic principles and destabilizing to our Republic. *Id.* . . .

THACKER, Circuit Judge, concurring: . . . I agree with the majority's conclusion that Appellees have standing to challenge the constitutionality of §2(c) of EO-2 and that EO-2 likely violates the Establishment Clause. However, in my view, we need not — and should not — reach this conclusion by relying on statements made by the President and his associates before inauguration.

While on the campaign trail, a non-incumbent presidential candidate has not yet taken the oath to "preserve, protect and defend the Constitution," U.S. Const. art. II, §1, and may speak to a host of promises merely to curry favor with the electorate. Once a candidate becomes President, however, the Constitution vests that individual with the awesome power of the executive office while simultaneously imposing constraints on that power. Thus, in undertaking the

Establishment Clause analysis, I believe we should focus our attention on conduct occurring on President Trump's inauguration date, January 20, 2017, and thereafter. Indeed, for the reasons below, looking to pre-inauguration conduct is neither advisable nor necessary. . . .

NIEMEYER, J., with whom SHEDD and AGEE, JJ., join, dissenting. . . .

II

In affirming the district court's ruling based on the Establishment Clause, the majority looks past the face of the Order's statements on national security and immigration, which it concedes are neutral in terms of religion, and considers campaign statements made by candidate Trump to conclude that the Order denigrates Islam, in violation of the Establishment Clause. This approach (1) plainly violates the Supreme Court's directive in *Mandel*; (2) adopts a *new rule of law* that uses campaign statements to recast the plain, unambiguous, and religiously neutral text of an executive order; and (3) radically extends the Supreme Court's Establishment Clause holdings. I address these legal errors in turn.

A

I begin with the majority's failure faithfully to apply *Mandel*. . . .

To reach its conclusion, the majority does not adopt the plaintiffs' broad argument that *Mandel* does not even apply. Instead, in its attempt to escape *Mandel*'s clear holding, it asserts that "[w]here plaintiffs have seriously called into question whether the stated reason for the challenged action was provided in good faith," the court may "step away from our deferential posture and look behind the stated reason for the challenged action" to attempt to discern the action's purpose. This approach, which totally undermines *Mandel*, is the foundation of its new rule that campaign statements may be considered to recast an unambiguous, later-adopted executive order on immigration. The majority states that even though the Order is on its face legitimate and provides reasons rooted in national security, because the plaintiffs "have more than plausibly alleged" bad faith, "we no longer defer" to the Order's stated purpose "and instead may 'look behind' [the Order]" in an attempt to discern whether the national security reason was *in fact* provided as a pretext for its religious purpose. This approach casually dismisses *Mandel, Fiallo* [v. *Bell*, 430 U.S. 787 (1977)], and *Din.*

If the majority's understanding had been shared by the Supreme Court, it would have compelled different results in each of *Mandel*, *Fiallo*, and *Din*, as in each of those cases the plaintiffs alleged bad faith with at least as much particularity as do the plaintiffs here. In *Mandel*, the allegations were such that Justice Marshall, writing in dissent, observed that "[e]ven the briefest peek behind the Attorney General's reason for refusing a waiver in this case would reveal that it is a sham." *Id.* at 778 (Marshall, J., dissenting). In *Fiallo*, Justice Marshall, again writing in dissent, pointed to the fact that the statute in question relied on "invidious classifications." *Fiallo*, 430 U.S. at 810 (Marshall, J., dissenting). And in *Din*, the plaintiffs argued that the consular decision should be reviewed because it fell within the "limited circumstances where the government provides no reason, or where the reason on its face is illegitimate." *Din*, 135 S. Ct. 2128. But, as those cases hold, a lack of good faith must appear on the face of the government's action, not from looking behind it. . . .

In looking behind the face of the government's action for facts to show the alleged bad faith, rather than looking for bad faith on the face of the executive action itself, the majority grants itself the power to conduct an extratextual search for evidence suggesting bad faith, which is exactly what three Supreme Court opinions have prohibited. *Mandel*, *Fiallo*, and *Din* have for decades been entirely clear that courts are not free to look behind these sorts of exercises of executive discretion in search of circumstantial evidence of alleged bad faith. The majority, now for the first time, rejects these holdings in favor of its politically desired outcome.

B

Considering the Order on its face, as we are required to do by *Mandel*, *Fiallo*, and *Din*, it is entirely without constitutional fault. The Order was a valid exercise of the President's authority under 8 U.S.C. §§1182(f) and 1185(a) to suspend the entry of "any aliens" or "any class of aliens" and to prescribe "reasonable rules, regulations, and orders" regarding entry, so long as the President finds that the aliens' admission would be "detrimental to the interests of the United States." And Executive Order No. 13,780 was not the first to be issued under this authority. Such orders were entered by Presidents Reagan, George H.W. Bush, Clinton, George W. Bush, and Obama. Moreover, the particular reasons given for the issuance of the Executive Order respond directly to the described risk of terrorism from six countries, justifying the

imposition of a 90-day pause in the admission of nationals from those
countries while the Administration determines whether existing
screening and vetting procedures are adequate. . . .

C

The majority's new rule, which considers statements made by
candidate Trump during the presidential campaign to conclude that the
Executive Order does not mean what it says, is fraught with danger and
impracticability. Apart from violating all established rules for construing
unambiguous texts — whether statutes, regulations, executive orders, or,
indeed, contracts — reliance on campaign statements to impose a new
meaning on an unambiguous Executive Order is completely strange to
judicial analysis.

The Supreme Court has repeatedly warned against "judicial
psychoanalysis of a drafter's heart of hearts." *McCreary Cty., Ky. v. Am.
Civil Liberties Union of Ky.*, 545 U.S. 844, 862 (2005). And consistent
with that warning, the Court has never, "in evaluating the legality of
executive action, deferred to comments made by such officials to the
media." *Hamdan v. Rumsfeld*, 548 U.S. 557, 623-24 n.52 (2006). The
Court's reluctance to consider statements made in the course of
campaigning derives from good sense and a recognition of the pitfalls
that would accompany such an inquiry.

Because of their nature, campaign statements are unbounded
resources by which to find intent of various kinds. They are often short-
hand for larger ideas; they are explained, modified, retracted, and
amplified as they are repeated and as new circumstances and arguments
arise. And they are often ambiguous. A court applying the majority's
new rule could thus have free reign to select whichever expression of a
candidate's developing ideas best supports its desired conclusion.

Moreover, opening the door to the use of campaign statements to
inform the text of later executive orders has no rational limit. If a court,
dredging through the myriad remarks of a campaign, fails to find
material to produce the desired outcome, what stops it from probing
deeper to find statements from a previous campaign, or from a previous
business conference, or from college?

And how would use of such statements take into account intervening
acts, events, and influences? When a candidate wins the election to the
presidency, he takes an oath of office to abide by the Constitution and
the laws of the Nation; he appoints officers of the government and retains
advisors, usually specialized in their field. Is there not the possibility that

a candidate might have different intentions than a President in office? And after taking office, a President faces new external events that may prompt new approaches altogether. How would a court assess the effect of these intervening events on presidential intent without conducting judicial psychoanalysis?

The foibles of such a rule are unbounded and its adoption would have serious implications for the democratic process. As Judge Kozinski said well when he wrote about the Ninth Circuit's use of the same campaign statements:

> Even if a politician's past statements were utterly clear and consistent, using them to yield a specific constitutional violation would suggest an absurd result — namely, that the policies of an elected official can be forever held hostage by the unguarded declarations of a candidate. If a court were to find that campaign skeletons prevented an official from pursuing otherwise constitutional policies, what could he do to cure the defect? Could he stand up and recant it all ("just kidding!") and try again? Or would we also need a court to police the sincerity of that mea culpa — piercing into the public official's "heart of hearts" to divine whether he really changed his mind, just as the Supreme Court has warned us not to? *See McCreary*, 545 U.S. at 862.

Washington v. Trump, No. 17-35105 (9th Cir. March 17, 2017) (Kozinski, J., dissenting from the denial of reconsideration en banc).

The danger of the majority's new rule is that it will enable any court to justify its decision to strike down any executive action with which it disagrees. It need only find one statement that contradicts the stated reasons for a subsequent executive action and thereby pronounce that reasons for the executive action are a pretext. This, I submit, is precisely what the majority opinion does.

Moreover, the unbounded nature of the majority's new rule will leave the President and his Administration in a clearly untenable position for future action. It is undeniable that President Trump will need to engage in foreign policy regarding majority-Muslim nations, including those designated by the Order. And yet the majority now suggests that at least some of those future actions might also be subject to the same challenges upheld today. Presumably, the majority does not intend entirely to stop the President from creating policies that address these nations, but it gives the President no guidelines for "cleansing" himself of the "taint" they have purportedly identified.

Finally, the new rule would by itself chill political speech directed at voters seeking to make their election decision. It is hard to imagine a greater or more direct chill on campaign speech than the knowledge that any statement made may be used later to support the inference of some nefarious intent when official actions are inevitably subjected to legal challenges. Indeed, the majority does not even deny that it employs an approach that will limit communication to voters. Instead, it simply opines remarkably that such chilling is "a welcome restraint."

The Supreme Court surely will shudder at the majority's adoption of this new rule that has no limits or bounds — one that transforms the majority's criticisms of a candidate's various campaign statements into a constitutional violation.

D

Finally, it is readily apparent that the plaintiffs' attempt to use campaign statements to transform a facially neutral executive action into an Establishment Clause violation would, in any event, be unlikely to succeed on the merits. . . .

The government here . . . provides ample nonreligious justification for the Order and actively contests that it has any religious purpose. Far from running "counter" to typical national security practice, each of the Order's six affected countries was previously designated as "a state sponsor of terrorism, has been significantly compromised by terrorist organizations, or contains active conflict zones." Order §1(d). And an Order that affects all nationals of six countries, irrespective of their religion, is not so precisely hewn to religious lines that we can infer, based on its operation alone, a predominantly religious purpose. . . .

* * *

For all of the foregoing reasons, I would reject the plaintiffs' and the district court's Establishment Clause arguments and vacate the district court's injunction.

SHEDD, Circuit Judge, with whom NIEMEYER and AGEE, JJ., join, dissenting. . . . [T]he district court's public interest analysis misses the mark. Here, the facially neutral Executive Order explains in detail the President's underlying reasoning for the temporary travel pause. Additionally, the record contains a joint letter from the Attorney General and Secretary of Homeland Security in which they detail their concerns "about weaknesses in our immigration system that pose a risk to our Nation's security," and in which they assert that "*it is imperative that we have a temporary pause on the entry of nationals from certain countries to allow this review to take place — a temporary pause that will immediately diminish the risk we face from application of our current vetting and screening programs for individuals seeking entry to the United States from these countries.*" [Italics in original.] To be sure, the district court found that the *President's* alleged bias is the primary reason for the temporary travel pause, but it found no such bias on the part of his Cabinet officials. Moreover, the district court acknowledged that national security is in fact a secondary reason for the temporary travel pause, and it found that the countries designated in the Executive Order present heightened security risks and that national security interests would be served by the temporary travel pause.

Despite this record, the district court — with no meaningful analysis — simply dismissed the public's interest in national security with the specious conclusion that "Defendants . . . have not shown, or even asserted, that national security cannot be maintained without an unprecedented six-country travel ban, a measure that has not been deemed necessary at any other time in recent history." *I.R.A.P. v. Trump*, —— F. Supp. 3d ——, ——, 2017 WL 1018235, *17 (D. Md. 2017). As noted, national security is the most compelling of public interests, and the question of how best to protect public safety in this area does not, as the district court implies, boil down to a least-restrictive means test, *Padilla v. Hanft*, 423 F.3d 386, 395 (4th Cir. 2005) ("We believe that the district court ultimately accorded insufficient deference to that determination, effectively imposing upon the President the equivalent of a least-restrictive-means test. To subject to such exacting scrutiny the President's determination that criminal prosecution would not adequately protect the Nation's security at a very minimum fails to accord the President the deference that is his when he acts pursuant to a broad delegation of authority from Congress."), or require a danger that satisfies the court's "independent foreign policy analysis," *Regan v. Wald*, 468 U.S. 222, 242 (1984). Therefore, the relevant point is not whether the temporary travel pause is the *only* way, or even the best way, to protect national security. The simple fact of the matter is that regardless of any ulterior motive one might ascribe to the President, the record still conclusively establishes that the temporary travel pause will in fact promote an important national security objective. . . .

[The dissenting opinion of AGEE, J., with whom NIEMEYER and SHEDD, JJ., join, is omitted.]

———————————

Hawaii v. Trump
United States Court of Appeals, Ninth Circuit, June 12, 2017
859 F.3d 741
cert. granted and stay applications granted in part,
137 S. Ct. 2080 (U.S. June 26, 2017) (per curiam)

[The court's treatment of the judicial reviewability of EO-1 in an earlier
phase of this litigation is excerpted at p. 1 in this *Supplement, supra.*]

PER CURIAM: We are asked to delineate the statutory and
constitutional limits to the President's power to control immigration in
this appeal of the district court's order preliminarily enjoining two
sections of Executive Order 13780 ("EO2" or "the Order"), "Protecting
the Nation From Foreign Terrorist Entry Into the United States." The
Immigration and Nationality Act ("INA") gives the President broad
powers to control the entry of aliens, and to take actions to protect the
American public. But immigration, even for the President, is not a one-
person show. The President's authority is subject to certain statutory and
constitutional restraints. We conclude that the President, in issuing the
Executive Order, exceeded the scope of the authority delegated to him by
Congress. In suspending the entry of more than 180 million nationals
from six countries, suspending the entry of all refugees, and reducing the
cap on the admission of refugees from 110,000 to 50,000 for the 2017
fiscal year, the President did not meet the essential precondition to
exercising his delegated authority: The President must make a sufficient
finding that the entry of these classes of people would be "detrimental to
the interests of the United States." Further, the Order runs afoul of other
provisions of the INA that prohibit nationality-based discrimination and
require the President to follow a specific process when setting the annual
cap on the admission of refugees. On these statutory bases, we affirm in
large part the district court's order preliminarily enjoining Sections 2 and
6 of the Executive Order.

I . . .

C

Two versions of a report from the Department of Homeland Security
("DHS") surfaced after EO1 issued. First, a draft report from DHS,
prepared about one month after EO1 issued and two weeks prior to
EO2's issuance, concluded that citizenship "is unlikely to be a reliable

indicator of potential terrorist activity" and that citizens of countries affected by EO1 are "[r]arely [i]mplicated in U.S.-[b]ased [t]errorism." Specifically, the DHS report determined that since the spring of 2011, at least eighty-two individuals were inspired by a foreign terrorist group to carry out or attempt to carry out an attack in the United States. Slightly more than half were U.S. citizens born in the United States, and the remaining persons were from twenty-six different countries — with the most individuals originating from Pakistan, followed by Somalia, Bangladesh, Cuba, Ethiopia, Iraq, and Uzbekistan. *Id.* Of the six countries included in EO2, only Somalia was identified as being among the "top" countries-of-origin for the terrorists analyzed in the report. During the time period covered in the report, three offenders were from Somalia; one was from Iran, Sudan, and Yemen each; and none was from Syria or Libya. The final version of the report, issued five days prior to EO2, concluded "that most foreign-born, [U.S.]-based violent extremists likely radicalized several years *after* their entry to the United States, [thus] limiting the ability of screening and vetting officials to prevent their entry because of national security concerns" (emphasis added).

The same day EO2 issued, Attorney General Jefferson B. Sessions III and Secretary of Homeland Security John F. Kelly submitted a letter to the President recommending that he "direct[ ] a temporary pause in entry" from countries that are "unable or unwilling to provide the United States with adequate information about their nationals" or are designated as "state sponsors of terrorism." . . .

IV . . .

B

We consider whether Plaintiffs are entitled to preliminary relief based on the likelihood that EO2 violates the INA. First, we address whether the President complied with the conditions set forth in §1182(f), which are necessary for invoking his authority. We next address the conflicts between EO2 and other provisions of the INA.

1

Under Article I of the Constitution, the power to make immigration laws "is entrusted exclusively to Congress." *Galvan v. Press*, 347 U.S. 522, 531 (1954); *see* U.S. Const. art. I, §8, cl. 4 ("The Congress shall have Power . . . [t]o establish an uniform Rule of Naturalization. . . .");

Fiallo v. Bell, 430 U.S. 787, 792 (1977) ("[O]ver no conceivable subject is the legislative power of Congress more complete than it is over the admission of aliens." (internal quotation marks omitted)); *id.* at 796 ("The conditions of entry for every alien, the particular classes of aliens that shall be denied entry altogether, the basis for determining such classification . . . have been recognized as matters solely for the responsibility of the Congress. . . ." (internal quotation marks omitted)). . . .

The parties dispute whether EO2 falls clearly within the President's congressionally delegated authority. To be sure, §1182(f) [*supra* p. 56 in this *Supplement*] gives the President broad authority to suspend the entry of aliens or classes of aliens. However, this authority is not unlimited. *Cf. Kent v. Dulles*, 357 U.S. 116, 129 (1958) ("[I]f that power is delegated, the standards must be adequate to pass scrutiny by the accepted tests."); *J.W. Hampton, Jr. & Co. v. United States*, 276 U.S. 394, 409 (1928) ("[L]egislative action is not a forbidden delegation of legislative power" if Congress provides an "intelligible principle to which the person or body authorized . . . is directed to conform."). Section 1182(f) requires that the President *find* that the entry of a class of aliens into the United States *would be detrimental* to the interests of the United States. This section requires that the President's findings support the conclusion that entry of all nationals from the six designated countries, all refugees, and refugees in excess of 50,000 would be harmful to the national interest. There is no sufficient finding in EO2 that the entry of the excluded classes would be detrimental to the interests of the United States.

i

Section 2(c) declares that "the unrestricted entry into the United States of nationals of Iran, Libya, Somalia, Sudan, Syria, and Yemen would be detrimental to the interests of the United States" and directs that the entry of nationals from those designated countries be barred for 90 days. 82 Fed. Reg. at 13213. The provision bans more than 180 million people from entry based on their national origin, including nationals who may have never been physically present in those countries. *See* Brief of Former National Security Officials as Amici Curiae, Dkt. No. 108 at 17. Section 2(c) states:

> [1] To temporarily reduce investigative burdens on relevant agencies during the review period [of the United States' vetting procedures], [2] to ensure the proper review and maximum utilization of available resources for the screening and vetting of foreign nationals, [3] to ensure that adequate

standards are established to prevent infiltration by foreign terrorists, and [4] in light of the national security concerns referenced in section 1 of this order, I hereby proclaim, pursuant to sections 212(f) and 215(a) of the INA, 8 U.S.C. [§§] 1182(f) [*supra* p. 56 in this *Supplement*] and 1185(a), that the unrestricted entry into the United States of nationals of Iran, Libya, Somalia, Sudan, Syria, and Yemen would be detrimental to the interests of the United States. I therefore direct that the entry into the United States of nationals of those six countries be suspended.

82 Fed. Reg. at 13213. The Government explains that the Order's objective "is to address the risk that potential terrorists might exploit possible weaknesses in the Nation's screening and vetting procedures while the review of those procedures is underway."

We reject the first three reasons provided in Section 2(c) because they relate to preservation of government resources to review existing procedures and ensure adequate vetting procedures. There is no finding that present vetting standards are inadequate, and no finding that absent the improved vetting procedures there likely will be harm to our national interests. These identified reasons do not support the conclusion that the entry of nationals from the six designated countries would be harmful to our national interests.

We turn to the fourth reason — national security concerns — and examine whether it confers a legally sufficient basis for the President's conclusion that the nationality-based entry restriction is warranted. Section 1(d) of the Order explains that nationals from Iran, Libya, Somalia, Sudan, Syria, and Yemen warrant additional scrutiny because:

> Each of these *countries* is a state sponsor of terrorism, has been significantly compromised by terrorist organizations, or contains active conflict zones. Any of these circumstances diminishes the foreign government's willingness or ability to share or validate important information about individuals seeking to travel to the United States. Moreover, the significant presence in each of these *countries* of terrorist organizations, their members, and others exposed to those organizations increases the chance that conditions will be exploited to enable terrorist operatives or sympathizers to travel to the United States. Finally, once foreign nationals from these countries are admitted to the United States, it is often difficult to remove them, because many of these *countries* typically delay issuing, or refuse to issue, travel documents.

Id. at 13210 (emphasis added).

Because of these country conditions, the Order concludes that "the risk of erroneously permitting entry of a national of one of these countries who intends to commit terrorist acts or otherwise harm the national security of the United States is unacceptably high." *Id.* at 13211. The Order further indicates that "hundreds of persons born abroad have been convicted of terrorism-related crimes in the United States[,]" but does not identify the number of nationals from the six designated countries who have been so convicted. *See id.* at 13212.

The Order makes no finding that nationality alone renders entry of this broad class of individuals a heightened security risk to the United States. *See Int'l Refugee Assistance Project*, —— F.3d at ——, 2017 WL 2273306, at *31 (Keenan, J., concurring in part and concurring in the judgment) ("[T]he Second Executive Order does not state that any *nationals* of the six identified countries, *by virtue of their nationality*, intend to commit terrorist acts in the United States or otherwise pose a detriment to the interests of the United States.").

The Order does not tie these nationals in any way to terrorist organizations within the six designated countries. It does not identify these nationals as contributors to active conflict or as those responsible for insecure country conditions. It does not provide any link between an individual's nationality and their propensity to commit terrorism or their inherent dangerousness. In short, the Order does not provide a rationale explaining why permitting entry of nationals from the six designated countries under current protocols would be detrimental to the interests of the United States.

The Order's discussion of country conditions fails to bridge the gap. Indeed, its use of nationality as the sole basis for suspending entry means that nationals without significant ties to the six designated countries, such as those who left as children or those whose nationality is based on parentage alone, should be suspended from entry. Yet, nationals of other countries who do have meaningful ties to the six designated countries — and may be contributing to the very country conditions discussed — fall outside the scope of Section 2(c). Consequently, EO2's focus on nationality "could have the paradoxical effect of barring entry by a Syrian national who has lived in Switzerland for decades, but not a Swiss national who has immigrated to Syria during its civil war." *Hawai'i TRO*, —— F. Supp.3d at ——, 2017 WL 1011673, at *15 (internal quotation marks and alterations omitted); *see also* Brief of the Cato Institute as Amicus Curiae, Dkt. No. 170 at 14–15 (providing statistics on nationals of the designated countries living in other countries as migrants, refugees, or asylum seekers and explaining that Syrian and Iranian nationals do not gain nationality by virtue of their place of birth). . . .

Finally, the Order relies on 8 U.S.C. §1187(a)(12) to explain why the six countries have been designated. 82 Fed. Reg. at 13210. In §1187(a)(12), Congress prevented use of the Visa Waiver Program by dual nationals of, or those who have visited in the last six years, (1) Iraq and Syria, (2) any country designated by the Secretary of State as a state sponsor of terrorism, and (3) any other country designated as a country of concern by the Secretary of Homeland Security, in consultation with the Secretary of State and the Director of National Intelligence. Rather than setting an outright ban on entry of nationals from these countries, Congress restricted access to the tourist Visa Waiver Program and instead required that persons who are nationals of or have recently traveled to these countries enter the United States with a visa. This provision reflects Congress's considered view on similar security concerns that the Order seeks to address. *See Chadha*, 462 U.S. at 951, 959 (explaining that our founders "consciously" chose to place the legislative process in the hands of a "deliberate and deliberative" body). The Order identifies no new information to justify Section 2(c)'s blanket ban as contrasted with §1187(a)(12)'s restriction from the Visa Waiver Program. Moreover, relying on §1187(a)(12) alone, which requires that aliens from these countries undergo vetting through visa procedures, does not explain why their *entry* would be detrimental to the interests of the United States. To the contrary, it effectively negates the Order's statement of detriment — that the "*unrestricted* entry into the United States of nationals [of the six designated countries] would be detrimental to the interests of the United States." 82 Fed. Reg. at 13213 (emphasis added). Section 1187(a)(12) dictates that the entry of individuals covered by the Order is never "unrestricted."

In conclusion, the Order does not offer a sufficient justification to suspend the entry of more than 180 million people on the basis of nationality. National security is not a "talismanic incantation" that, once invoked, can support any and all exercise of executive power under §1182(f). *United States v. Robel*, 389 U.S. 258, 263-64 (1967); *see also Korematsu v. United States*, 323 U.S. 214, 235 (1944) (Murphy, J., dissenting) ("[T]he exclusion order necessarily must rely for its reasonableness upon the assumption that all persons of Japanese ancestry may have a dangerous tendency to commit sabotage and espionage and to aid our Japanese enemy in other ways. It is difficult to believe that reason, logic or experience could be marshalled in support of such an assumption."). Section 1182(f) requires that the President exercise his authority only after meeting the precondition of finding that entry of an alien or class of aliens *would be* detrimental to the interests of the United States. Here, the President has not done so.

ii . . . .

[The Court found that EO2's suspension of travel of refugees into the
United States under USRAP [U.S. Refugee Admissions Program, a
consortium of federal agencies that identify and admit refugees for
resettlement] and of decisions on applications for refugee status for 120
days is not supported by any evidence that the entry of refugees in the
interim time period would be detrimental to the interests of the United
States.] . . . .

iii . . . .

[The court found that the 50,000 cap on entry of refugees for fiscal
2017 is unsupported by evidence that entry in excess of the cap would be
detrimental to the interests of the United States.] . . . .

2 . . . .

The Government tries to reconcile the Order's Section 2(c) with
§1152(a)(1)(A) by arguing that Section 2(c) bars *entry* of nationals from
the six designated countries but does not deny the *issuance of immigrant
visas* based on nationality. EO2's suspension of entry on the basis of
nationality, however, in substance operates as a ban on visa issuance on
the basis of nationality. . . . Indeed, the Government clarified at oral
argument that as a practical matter, the entry ban would be implemented
through visa denials. . . .

We cannot blind ourselves to the fact that, for nationals of the six
designated countries, EO2 is effectively a ban on the issuance of
immigrant visas. If allowed to stand, EO2 would bar issuance of visas
based on nationality in violation of §1152(a)(1)(A). The Government did
not dispute this point at oral argument, and it stands to reason that the
whole system of the visa issuance would grind to a halt for nationals of
the six designated countries whose entry is barred from the United States.
Issuance of visas will automatically stop for those who are banned based
on nationality. Yet Congress could not have used "more explicit
language" in "unambiguously direct[ing] that no nationality-based
discrimination shall occur." *Legal Assistance for Vietnamese Asylum
Seekers*, 45 F.3d at 473. . . .

Under the Government's argument, the President could circumvent
the limitations set by §1152(a)(1)(A) by permitting the issuance of visas
to nationals of the six designated countries, but then deny them entry.

Congress could not have intended to permit the President to flout §1152(a) so easily. *See Dada v. Mukasey*, 554 U.S. 1, 16 (2008) (courts should not read statutes in such a way that renders them a "nullity" or is "unsustainable"). . . .

Having considered the President's authority under § 1182(f) and the non-discrimination mandate of §1152(a)(1)(A), we also conclude that Plaintiffs have shown a likelihood of success on the merits of their claim that Section 2(c) of the Order, in suspending the issuance of immigrant visas and denying entry based on nationality, exceeds the restriction of §1152(a)(1)(A) and the overall statutory scheme intended by Congress. . . .

5

Finally, we note that in considering the President's authority, we are cognizant of Justice Jackson's tripartite framework in *Youngstown Sheet & Tube Co. v. Sawyer*. *See* 343 U.S. 579, 635-38 (1952) (Jackson, J., concurring). Section 1182(f) ordinarily places the President's authority at its maximum. "When the President acts pursuant to an express or implied authorization of Congress, his authority is at its maximum, for it includes all that he possesses in his own right plus all that Congress can delegate." *Id.* at 635. However, given the express will of Congress through §1152(a)(1)(A)'s non-discrimination mandate, §1157's procedure for refugee admissions to this country, and §1182(a)(3)(B)'s criteria for determining terrorism-related inadmissibility, the President took measures that were incompatible with the expressed will of Congress, placing his power "at its lowest ebb." *Id.* at 637. In this zone, "Presidential claim to a power at once so conclusive and preclusive must be scrutinized with caution, for what is at stake is the equilibrium established by our constitutional system." *Id.* at 638. We have based our decision holding the entry ban unlawful on statutory considerations, and nothing said herein precludes Congress and the President from reaching a new understanding and confirming it by statute. If there were such consensus between Congress and the President, then we would view Presidential power at its maximum, and not in the weakened state based on conflict with statutory law. *See id.* at 635-38. . . .

VI

We affirm in part and vacate in part the district court's preliminary injunction order. As to the remaining Defendants, we affirm the injunction as to Section 2(c), suspending entry of nationals from the six designated countries for 90 days; Section 6(a), suspending USRAP for 120 days; and Section 6(b), capping the entry of refugees to 50,000 in the fiscal year 2017. We vacate the portions of the injunction that prevent the Government from conducting internal reviews, as otherwise directed in Sections 2 and 6, and the injunction to the extent that it runs against the President. We remand the case to the district court with instructions to re-issue a preliminary injunction consistent with this opinion.

Affirmed in part; vacated in part; and remanded with instructions. . . .

NOTES AND QUESTIONS

1. *Stays.* The Supreme Court granted certiorari in both of the foregoing cases and granted the stay applications in part, "to the extent the injunctions prevent enforcement of §2(c) with respect to foreign nationals who lack any bona fide relationship with a person or entity in the United States." 137 S. Ct. at 2087. But it left the injunctions entered by the lower courts in place with respect to respondents and those similarly situated — permanent resident aliens and others with the posited bona fide relationships. Why the difference? What is a "bona fide relationship"? Compare *United States v. Verdugo-Urquidez*, 494 U.S. 259 (1990), NSL p. 226, CTL p. 36. Will the distinction the Court has drawn increase or decrease litigation about the scope of the stay? The Administration moved quickly to give its own definition of "bona fide relationship." *See* Gardiner Harris and Ron Nixon, *Stepsister, Yes; Grandma, No: U.S. Sets Guidelines for Revised Travel Ban*, N.Y. Times, June 28, 2017. Is its definition now controlling or is the Supreme Court's?

2. *Standing.* In the litigation challenging the travel bans, the government "rounded up the usual suspects" preventing judicial review, variously raising standing, justiciability, and ripeness challenges to the lawsuits. We have omitted the courts' discussions of plaintiffs' standing in the excerpted cases, in part because they both included plaintiffs whose travel was directly curtailed by the travel bans and therefore easily

satisfied the injury-in-fact requirement for standing. But how did the *states* have standing? One theory was "based on [the states'] quasi-sovereign interests, as *parens patriae*, to secure its residents from the harmful effects of discrimination." *Hawaii*, 859 F.3d at 765 n.6. The court dodged this potentially sweeping theory, however, in favor of finding standing based on the states' *own* proprietary interests. What were those interests?

3. *Justiciability.* The government made a double-barreled attack on justiciability (which the Ninth Circuit called "reviewability" in *Washington v. Trump, supra* p. 1 in this *Supplement*). First, it argued for "consular nonreviewability," the doctrine that a decision to issue or withhold a visa is not subject to judicial review. *See Li Hing of Hong Kong, Inc. v. Levin,* 800 F.2d 970, 971 (9th Cir. 1986) ("[I]t has been consistently held that the consular official's decision to issue or withhold a visa is not subject either to administrative or judicial review."). Given the sweep of EO-2, and the constitutional bases of some of plaintiffs' claims, can you rebut this argument? *See Hawaii*, 859 F.3d at 768 ("Plaintiffs do not seek review of an individual consular officer's decision to grant or to deny a visa pursuant to valid regulations, which could implicate the consular nonreviewability doctrine. Plaintiffs instead challenge 'the President's *promulgation* of sweeping immigration policy.' Courts can and do review both constitutional and statutory 'challenges to the substance and implementation of immigration policy.'") (internal citations omitted). Second, the government argued that the President's immigration decisions, *particularly when motivated by national security concerns*, were unreviewable. Do the national security cases you have read elsewhere in the casebook support such a claim? Is it consistent with what you understand to be the constitutional structure? *See Washington v. Trump, supra* p. 1 in this *Supplement* (holding no).

Even if such claims of nonreviewability are too sweeping, should they bear on what evidence the courts may consider and how much deference they owe the executive in these cases?

4. *The Statutory Claims.* As our brief excerpt from the INA suggests, *supra* p. 56 in this *Supplement*, plaintiffs had a colorable statutory claim based on the INA's non-discrimination provision, §1152(a)(1)(A). Why didn't the majority in *IRAP* avoid the issues raised by the constitutional claim and decide the case on the basis of the statutory claim? If they had reached the statutory claim, is there any statutory rebuttal the

government could have made? (Hint: compare the scope of EO-2 and the authority delegated to the executive by §1182(f) with the scope of the nondiscrimination provision.)

5. *The Establishment Clause Claim.* The majority and the dissenters in the en banc Fourth Circuit in *IRAP* disagreed primarily about the meaning of *Mandel*. What was the disagreement? Was *Mandel's* reference to "a facially legitimate *and* bona fide reason" (emphasis added) a throw-away line or an invitation to courts to look behind the text of an executive order in order to ascertain its purpose? If a court can look behind the text, where does it look? Comments by the President? By other members of the executive branch? Which ones? How formal and how nearly contemporaneous must they be? Statements by a presidential candidate during the campaign?

If you are inclined to consider the evidence that the *IRAP* majority considered (basically, all of the above), won't you inevitably be selective? Can we trust a court not to cherry-pick such evidence? Does this over-empower the courts, and could it chill electoral campaigns, as the dissenters suggest?

On the other hand, suppose you look just at the text of the executive order, as the government suggested that courts must. If the court upholds an order on that basis, even though the President tweets, "I just told my lawyers to say anything, but this is the ban on Muslims that I promised," would the strictly textual approach to deciding the constitutional challenge undermine the authority and credibility of the courts by forcing them to accept admitted pretext? *See generally* Josh Blackman, *Analysis of IRAP v. Trump, Parts I-V*, Lawfare, May-June 2017, and Alex Loomis, *Will the Supreme Court Consider the Risk of Trump's Post-Ruling Tweets?*, Lawfare, June 6, 2017. Which outcome is worse? Does Judge Thacker's concurring opinion offer a viable middle path? What is it?

6. *Lost in Litigation: the Policy Question.* Is banning Muslims, or even just travelers from the six Muslim-majority countries named in EO-2, good anti-terrorist policy? Consider both the DHS reports cited in *Hawaii, supra,* and the practical problems and costs and benefits of profiling discussed in the casebook (NSL pp. 820-826, CTL pp. 448-454), as well as the likely impact on Muslim immigrant communities *already* legally resident in the United States. Is there any way other than a ban to reduce the likelihood that dangerous persons will enter the United States from areas that are experiencing serious terrorist violence?

(Does EO-2 actually chose another way, instead of a ban?) If you have read *Korematsu v. United States*, 323 U.S. 214 (1944) (NSL p. 889, CTL p. 517), you'll recognize this as a variant on a question posed by *Korematsu*: was there any way other than wholesale internment to reduce any threat to national security posed by Japanese nationals in the United States during World War II?

————————

[NSL p. 874; CTL p. 502. Insert new Note 6.]

6. *Undocumented Immigrants and the Suspension Clause.* Although the Supreme Court in *Boumediene* appeared to assume that the Suspension Clause protects non-citizens within the United States, the Third Circuit held otherwise in *Castro v. U.S. Dep't of Homeland Security*, 835 F.3d 422 (3d Cir. 2016), concluding that undocumented immigrants "apprehended within hours of surreptitiously entering the United States" are functionally equivalent to "arriving aliens . . . stopped at the border," and that such arriving non-citizens are not constitutionally entitled to habeas review even after — and notwithstanding — *Boumediene*. *See id.* at 445-449 & n.22. (In so holding, the Court of Appeals upheld a statute that took away federal habeas jurisdiction in such cases.) Indeed, the court held that *Boumediene*'s multi-factor test "provide[s] little guidance" for the constitutional entitlement to habeas within the United States because "the Court derived the factors from its extraterritoriality jurisprudence in order to assess the reach of the Suspension Clause to a territory where the United States is not sovereign." *Id.* at 445 n.25. "In our case, of course, there is no question that Petitioners were apprehended within the sovereign territory of the United States; thus, the *Boumediene* factors are of limited utility in determining Petitioners' entitlement to the protections of the Suspension Clause." *Id.*

But aren't *Boumediene*'s factors of limited utility because there's a *stronger* case for habeas for persons already within the United States at the time of their detention? *See* Steve Vladeck, *Third Circuit Holds Suspension Clause Does Not Apply to Non-Citizens Physically (But Not Lawfully) Present in the United States*, Just Security, Aug. 29, 2016. What, after all, is the argument for why non-citizen terrorism suspects captured overseas (and who have never set foot on U.S. soil) are protected by the Suspension Clause, but undocumented immigrants arrested within the territorial United States — or even those stopped at the border — are not?

And do you suspect that the Court of Appeals would differentiate between an undocumented immigrant who was "apprehended within hours of surreptitiously entering the United States" and one arrested months (if not years) later? If so, where is the line? Is that line established by the Constitution's text?

These concerns could have made *Castro* a compelling case for Supreme Court review. But over no recorded dissents, the Justices denied certiorari on April 17, 2017. *See Castro v. U.S. Dep't of Homeland Security*, 137 S. Ct. 1581 (2017) (mem.). Thus, in the Third Circuit at least, it appears that the Suspension Clause may not protect many (if not most) undocumented immigrants even when arrested on U.S. soil — especially those arrested within a short period of time after their entry into the United States.

[NSL p. 954; CTL p. 582. Insert new Note 4.]

4. *President Trump and Guantánamo*. By the time President Obama left office on January 20, 2017, the remaining detainee population at Guantánamo had been whittled down to 41 men, five of whom had been approved for transfer under the PRB process described in Note 3, *supra*. In contrast to his predecessor, however, President Trump campaigned on a commitment to reinvigorate military detention at Guantánamo. To that end, media reports early in 2017 shared the language of multiple draft executive orders apparently designed to carry out that pledge — and to repeal and repudiate at least some of President Obama's Guantánamo-related initiatives. *See, e.g.*, Charlie Savage, *ISIS Detainees May Be Held at Guantánamo, Document Shows*, N.Y. Times, Feb. 9, 2017. But as of early July 2017, no such executive orders had been issued, and no new detainees had been sent to Guantánamo. Why do you suppose that there was so little movement on one of the President's major campaign issues?

[NSL p. 979; CTL p. 607. Replace Note 8 with the following Note.]

8. *The Supreme Court Steps In*. On June 19, 2017, the Supreme Court reversed the Second Circuit's decision in part and vacated it in part. *See Ziglar v. Abbasi*, 137 S. Ct. 1843 (2017). Writing for a 4-2 majority (Justices Sotomayor, Kagan, and Gorsuch did not participate), Justice Kennedy rejected the Second Circuit's recognition of *Bivens* claims for damages for the plaintiffs' alleged constitutional violations,

holding that courts should stay their hand before recognizing damages remedies for constitutional violations by federal officers in contexts in which the Supreme Court had not previously approved them. *See id.* at 1858-1863. The Court therefore threw out the plaintiffs' claims of an unconstitutional "detention policy" against all of the defendants, and returned the plaintiffs' claims of unconstitutional "prisoner abuse" against Warden Hasty to the Court of Appeals for proper consideration of whether it presented a "new context." *See id.* at 1863-1865. As for the plaintiffs' 42 U.S.C. §1985 civil conspiracy claims, the majority held that the officer-defendants were entitled to qualified immunity because "the conspiracy . . . is alleged to have been between or among officers in the same branch of the Government (the Executive Branch) and in the same Department (the Department of Justice)," and because "the discussions were the preface to, and the outline of, a general and far-reaching policy," neither of which had previously been held to provide a basis for liability under §1985. *See id.* at 1867.

Ziglar therefore wipes off the books — but does not affirmatively repudiate — the Second Circuit's prior discussion of whether qualified immunity barred the plaintiffs' constitutional claims. If you were a district or circuit judge within that jurisdiction in a future case, how persuasive would you find that analysis? Put another way, what kind of precedent do *Turkmen* and *Ziglar* actually set for legal constraints on the actions of government officers (or the lack thereof) in the aftermath of the next terrorist attack on U.S. soil?

[NSL p. 1010, CTL p. 638. Insert at end of Note 2 before "a. *What Conduct Is Covered?*"]

In the boxed excerpt of the War Crimes Act, 18 U.S.C. §2441, we omitted the *statutory* definition of "Common Article 3 violations." *Id.* §2441(d). A "grave breach of Common Article 3" is defined there expressly to include torture, cruel or inhuman treatment, performing biological experiments, murder, mutilation or maiming, intentionally causing serious bodily injury, rape, sexual assault or abuse, and taking hostages. Common Article 3 does not expressly condemn grave breaches. *See* NSL p. 280, CTL p. 104. Article 130 of the Third Geneva Convention and Article 147 of the Fourth Geneva Convention (NSL p. 286, CTL p. 110), however, both define grave breaches as including "wilful killing, torture or inhuman treatment, including biological experiments, wilfully causing great suffering or serious injury to body or health." Which definition affords greater protection to noncombatants?

_____

[NSL p. 1014, CTL p. 642. Insert at the end of Note 3.]

As part of the National Defense Authorization Act for Fiscal Year 2016, Pub. L. No. 114-92, 129 Stat. 726 (2015), Congress enacted what has become known as the McCain-Feinstein Amendment, which, like the Detainee Treatment Act, seeks to limit U.S. interrogations to methods that are listed in Army Field Manual 2-22.3 Unlike the Detainee Treatment Act, the McCain-Feinstein Amendment applies to any "officer, employee, or other agent of the United States government" (outside of the law enforcement context), and limits the interrogation methods that can be deployed against any individual "detained within a facility owned, operated, or controlled by a department or agency of the United States in any armed conflict." *Id.* §1045(a)(2)(B), 129 Stat. at 977. And presumably to avoid the prospect of constant (and secret) rewritings of the Manual to accommodate new (and pernicious) techniques, the McCain-Feinstein Amendment further provides that the Manual can be revised "[n]ot sooner than three years after the date of enactment of this Act, and once every three years thereafter." *Id.* §1045(a)(6)(A), 129 Stat. at 978. Moreover, any such revisions must be "made available to the public 30 days prior to the date the revisions take effect." *Id.*

Do you see why, given the lessons of the past 15-plus years, Congress would gravitate toward this approach — limiting the methods that can be used, without regard to their physical or psychological manifestations and without having the legality turn in any way on the statutory, constitutional, or international law rights of the subjects? Does this approach seem less open to the kinds of interpretive complexities surveyed in this chapter? Is there any argument that preventing the President from revising the Army Field Manual (and from thereby expanding the permissible array of interrogation methods) except on a regular, three-year schedule raises constitutional concerns?

[NSL p. 1037, CTL p. 665. Add to Note 1.]

Efforts to obtain public release of the full 6,700-page Senate report have not been successful. The Senate Select Committee on Intelligence sent copies of the entire report to at least eight federal agencies and asked that they incorporate the report into their records. Doing so would have made the documents subject to Freedom of Information Act requests. After the agencies refused to add the report to their records, the ACLU sued the CIA and argued that the report was nevertheless an "agency record" subject to FOIA. Mark Mazzetti, Matthew Rosenberg & Charlie Savage, *Trump Administration Returns Copies of Report on CIA Torture to Congress*, N.Y. Times, June 2, 2017. In May 2016, the D.C. Circuit ruled that the Senate report remains a congressional document and is not subject to disclosure under FOIA. *ACLU v. CIA*, 823 F.3d 655 (D.C. Cir. 2016), *cert. denied*, 137 S. Ct. 1837 (2017).

Meanwhile, counsel for Guantánamo detainees filed motions in at least four cases requesting that the SSCI report be preserved, and the government deposited a copy of the report with a federal district court for the District of Columbia in connection with Abd al-Rahim al-Nashiri's habeas corpus lawsuit. Quinta Jurecic, *DOJ Delivered Only Copy of SSCI Report to Court, Senate Democrats Write*, Lawfare, Mar. 13, 2017. However, the Trump administration has begun returning to Congress its copies of the full SSCI report. These copies could be retained by the Senate indefinitely, or even destroyed. Mazzetti, Rosenberg & Savage, *supra*. See *infra* this *Supplement* pp. 108-109.

[NSL p. 1047, CTL p. 675. Add to Note 3.]

On October 21, 2016, the Fourth Circuit vacated the district court's dismissal and reinstated the case. *Al Shimari v. CACI Premier Tech., Inc.*, 840 F.3d 147 (4th Cir. 2016). The appellate court held that a challenge to conduct by CACI employees that was unlawful when committed is justiciable, irrespective of whether that conduct occurred under the actual control of the military.

As noted at NSL p. 1038/CTL p. 666, Note 6, the CIA relied on contract psychologists to develop and implement the early stages of the interrogation program based on techniques adapted from the SERE school. Litigation by three former detainees, one of whom died in CIA custody, against CIA contract psychologists James E. Mitchell and Bruce Jessen under the ATS is ongoing at this writing. Two motions to dismiss have been denied in federal district court in the Eastern District of Washington. In April 2016 and January 2017, the court found no bar to justiciability based on the political question doctrine or sovereign immunity. The court found jurisdiction for the lawsuit under the ATS and ruled that the defendants have not met their burden of showing that they were "agents" of the United States within the meaning of a Military Commissions Act (MCA) provision that bars such lawsuits in certain instances. *Salim v. Mitchell*, 183 F. Supp. 3d 1121 (W.D. Wash. 2016); *Salim v. Mitchell*, No. CV-15-0286-JLQ, 2017 WL 390270 (W.D. Wash. Jan. 27, 2017).

Although the lawsuit was scheduled for trial in late 2017, in March 2017 CIA Director Michael Pompeo formally asserted the state secrets privilege to prevent disclosure of seven categories of information concerning the CIA interrogation program, and to prevent the deposition of three CIA officers. James Risen, Sheri Fink & Charlie Savage, *State Secrets Privilege Invoked to Block Testimony in CIA Torture Case*, N.Y. Times, Mar. 8, 2017. However, the government did not seek dismissal of the lawsuit when making its state secrets privilege motion, and plaintiffs' attorney stated that the case can proceed on the public record. *CIA Asserts State Secrets Privilege in Torture Case*, Secrecy News, Mar. 9, 2017.

One lawsuit filed on behalf of former prisoners has produced chilling testimony about the interrogation techniques. *See* Sheri Fink & James Risen, *Psychologists Open a Window on Brutal C.I.A. Interrogations,* N.Y. Times, June 21, 2017. The companion video is available at https://www.nytimes.com/interactive/2017/06/20/us/cia-torture.html?_r=0.

[NSL p. 1064, CTL p. 692. Add at the end of Note 1.]

A statute prescribing punishment for treason tracks the language of the Constitution:

> Whoever, owing allegiance to the United States, levies war against them or adheres to their enemies, giving them aid and comfort within the United States or elsewhere, is guilty of treason and shall suffer death, or shall be imprisoned not less than five years and fined under this title but not less than $10,000; and shall be incapable of holding any office under the United States. [18 U.S.C. §2381 (2012).]

At this writing in early summer 2017, both congressional intelligence committees and a Special Counsel were investigating allegations that officials in the Donald Trump presidential campaign colluded with Russia to influence the November 2016 election in Trump's favor. Some argued that any such collusion would amount to treason. *See, e.g.*, Nicholas Kristof, Op-ed., *"There's a Smell of Treason in the Air,"* N.Y. Times, Mar. 23, 2017.

One of us responded that such arguments were groundless, because "[w]hatever one thinks of Russia, Vladimir Putin, or the current state of relations between it/them and the United States, we are not at war with Russia. Full stop. Russia is therefore not an 'enemy' of the United States. Full stop." Steve Vladeck, *[Calling It] Treason Doth Never Prosper . . .* , Just Security, Mar. 24, 2017. But the terms "war" and "enemy" are not defined in either the Constitution or the treason statute. So what sources should we (and, more importantly, courts) look to in deciding the meaning of these terms?

At least during World War II, courts held that individuals could commit "treason" only during the existence of formally declared hostilities against an identified enemy. *See, e.g., United States v. McWilliams*, 54 F. Supp. 791, 793 (D.D.C. 1944) ("The averments as to what happened between 1933 and 1940 cannot be deemed a charge of conspiracy to commit treason since an essential element therein is aid and comfort to 'enemies' and Germany did not become a statutory enemy until December 1941."); *see also* Steve Vladeck, *We Have Met the Enemy, and He Is . . . ?*, Just Security, Mar. 25, 2017 (arguing that liability under the treason statute requires "the existence of an armed conflict under both domestic and international law — something noticeably lacking with regard to the United States and Russia").

While it is true that the United States is not "at war" with Russia in the same sense that we were with France in 1800 (see *Bas v. Tingy*, 4 U.S. (4 Dall.) 37 (1800) (NSL p. 109)), relations between our two countries appear to be extremely adversarial. Some might even paraphrase Justice Bushrod Washington to the effect that, if Russia is not our enemy, we know not what constitutes an enemy.

Should prosecution for treason be possible only if the United States is engaged in a shooting war with a state to which one gives "aid and comfort"? Would someone owing allegiance to the United States who gives aid and comfort to ISIS be guilty of treason? Put another way, should the statute (and Constitution) require any or all of (1) an armed conflict (2) declared (or otherwise authorized) by Congress (3) against a nation-state? What are the best arguments for and against each of these requirements?

[NSL p. 1094, CTL p. 722. Add new Note 9.]

9. *The Article I Question.* One last point that has largely gone overlooked in debates about the constitutionality of extraterritorial assertions of criminal jurisdiction is the scope of Congress's regulatory power to punish conduct undertaken by non-citizens overseas. Although the Constitution gives Congress the power to "define and punish . . . offenses against the law of nations," U.S. Const. art. I, §8, cl. 10, many of the offenses over which Congress has conferred extraterritorial criminal jurisdiction (such as the material support statutes described above) are not, in fact, "offenses against the law of nations." In those cases, the most likely source of Congress's regulatory power is the so-called Foreign Commerce Clause, which empowers Congress "[t]o regulate commerce with foreign nations," *id.* cl. 3, and which lower courts have "construed . . . expansively, to permit Congress to regulate economic activity abroad if it has a substantial effect on this Nation's foreign commerce." *Baston v. United States*, 137 S. Ct. 850, 850 (2017) (Thomas, J., dissenting from the denial of certiorari).

But the Supreme Court has never specifically addressed "Congress' power to regulate, or even criminalize, conduct within another nation's sovereign territory," *id.* at 852, and most of the key lower-court precedents are based upon an expansive understanding of the *Interstate Commerce Clause* that the Supreme Court has since rejected. *See id.* ("[E]ven if the foreign commerce power were broader than the interstate commerce power as understood at the founding, it would not follow that the foreign commerce power is broader than the interstate commerce power as this Court now construes it."). This has led Justice Thomas, at least, to conclude that, "whatever the correct interpretation of the foreign commerce power may be, it does not confer upon Congress a virtually plenary power over global economic activity," *id.* at 853, and to urge his colleagues to revisit the issue in an appropriate case. *See id.*

Given the materials in this chapter, would the material support statutes present such an appropriate case, or is it clear to you that the knowing provision of material support to a terrorist (18 U.S.C. §2339A) or designated foreign terrorist organization (*id.* §2339B) will always have a sufficient connection to foreign commerce to satisfy Article I?

_____

[NSL p. 1192, CTL p. 820. Insert before Note 1.]

In *Al Bahlul v. United States* ("*Al Bahlul III*"), 840 F.3d 757 (D.C. Cir. 2016) (en banc) (per curiam), *petition for cert. filed*, No. 16-1307 (U.S. Mar. 28, 2017), a fractured Court of Appeals sided with Judge Henderson's panel dissent in *Al Bahlul II* and affirmed Al Bahlul's conspiracy conviction — although no single rationale commanded a majority. Nine judges (all of the court's active judges, except Chief Judge Garland and Judge Srinivasan) participated in the decision.

Of those nine, six voted to affirm — four (Judges Brown, Griffith, Henderson, and Kavanaugh) on the ground that, "consistent with Articles I and III of the Constitution, Congress may make conspiracy to commit war crimes an offense triable by military commission." *Id.* at 758. Judges Millett and Wilkins, whose votes were necessary to form the majority, voted to affirm on narrower grounds — the former because of her conclusion that Al Bahlul forfeited his jurisdictional challenge, and that his conspiracy conviction was not plainly erroneous; the latter because "the particular features of Bahlul's conviction demonstrate that Bahlul was not convicted of an inchoate conspiracy offense," but rather of conspiracy to commit a completed war crime — on a theory of "joint criminal enterprise" recognized by international criminal law. *See id.* Three judges (Rogers, Tatel, and Pillard) jointly dissented, largely for the reasons set forth in the *Al Bahlul II* panel opinion excerpted above.

Note several curious features of this split result:

First, the absence of a majority rationale leaves the major constitutional question — whether the military commissions may try offenses that are not international war crimes — at least formally unsettled. And becauuse the D.C. Circuit's ruling in *Al Bahlul III* leaves intact the Court of Military Commission Review's conclusion that the commissions may try such offenses, it is likely that the commissions will proceed on the assumption that they may continue to try such crimes, until and unless the matter is decisively settled to the contrary.

Second, the absence of a majority rationale may also weaken the imperative for the Supreme Court to intervene, at least at this point, since either of the narrower grounds offered by Judges Millett and Wilkins might provide enough of a reason for the Justices to believe that Al Bahlul's case, specifically, would not allow them to reach the major constitutional question. Indeed, one does not have to agree with either of the narrow concurrences (both of which are open to some fairly substantial critiques, *see* Steve Vladeck, *Al Bahlul and the Long Shadow*

of Illegitimacy, Lawfare, Oct. 22, 2016), to believe that they complicate
the case for further review.

Thus, as you consider the following Notes and Questions (written
with an eye toward the panel decision in *Al Bahlul II*), keep in mind what
Judge Kavanaugh argued in his concurrence in *Al Bahlul III*:

> The question of whether conspiracy may constitutionally be tried by
> military commission is extraordinarily important and deserves a "definitive
> answer." The question implicates an important part of the U.S.
> Government's war strategy. And other cases in the pipeline require a clear
> answer to the question. This case unfortunately has been pending in this
> Court for more than five years. It is long past time for us to resolve the issue
> squarely and definitively. [840 F.3d at 760 n.1 (Kavanaugh, J., concurring).]

Whatever you think the answer to this question actually is, isn't Judge
Kavanaugh absolutely right that it's long past-time that the matter be
settled? At this writing, a petition for certiorari in the Supreme Court was
pending — with some of the *amici* making exactly this point in urging
the Justices to step in. *See* Brief of the National Institute of Military
Justice as *Amicus Curiae* in Support of the Petitioner, *Al Bahlul v. United
States*, No. 16-1307 (U.S. filed May 31, 2017), *available at*
https://perma.cc/4A5J-AALD. Would you vote to grant certiorari in *Al
Bahlul* regardless (or, indeed, because) of how you would answer the
merits question? Why or why not?

[NSL p. 1194, CTL p. 822. Replace Note 6.]

6. *War Crimes Without a War?* Another major jurisdictional
challenge to the commissions has been lodged by Abd al-Rahim al-
Nashiri, a Guantánamo detainee charged with a number of offenses,
including involvement in the 2000 bombing of the USS *Cole*. *See In re
al-Nashiri* (*"al-Nashiri I"*), 791 F.3d 71 (D.C. Cir. 2015). Al-Nashiri,
like Bahlul, asserts that the offenses with which he has been charged
were not recognized as international war crimes at the time of their
commission — not, as in *Al Bahlul*, because international law doesn't
recognize the offenses in the abstract, but because, in Al-Nashiri's view
anyway, the United States was not actually engaged in an armed conflict
with Al Qaeda at the time of the bombing, *i.e.*, prior to September 11,
2001.

If the jurisdiction of the commissions does indeed turn on the
existence of a state of armed conflict at the time of the relevant offense

(which even Judge Henderson concedes in her *Al Bahlul II* dissent, and which the Military Commissions Act itself appears to require, *see* 10 U.S.C. §§948a(9), 950p(c)), what is the argument for the assertion of jurisdiction over Al-Nashiri?

As a matter of U.S. domestic and international humanitarian law, when did the non-international armed conflict with Al Qaeda begin? In 2014, the district court declined to answer that question in the context of a pretrial habeas petition, holding that it should abstain in favor of the military commission — and a potential postconviction appeal. *See Al-Nashiri v. Obama*, 76 F. Supp. 3d 218 (D.D.C. 2014). A divided panel of the D.C. Circuit affirmed in 2016, concluding that (1) abstention was warranted from a pre-trial habeas challenge to the military's assertion of jurisdiction over particular *offenses* (as opposed to challenges to its jurisdiction based upon the *status* of the defendant); and (2) because his jurisdictional challenge presented a question of first impression, Nashiri could not meet the high bar for a writ of mandamus. *See In re Al-Nashiri* (*"al-Nashiri II"*), 835 F.3d 110 (D.C. Cir. 2016). As of this writing, a petition for certiorari was pending before the Supreme Court. *See Al-Nashiri v. Trump*, No. 16-8966 (U.S. filed Jan. 17, 2017).

[NSL p. 1224, CTL p. 852. Replace "Interstate Quarantine Regulations" with the following.]

Interstate Quarantine Regulations
42 C.F.R. pt. 70 (effective Feb. 21, 2017)

§70.2 Measures in the Event of Inadequate Local Control.

Whenever the Director of the Centers for Disease Control and Prevention determines that the measures taken by health authorities of any State or possession (including political subdivisions thereof) are insufficient to prevent the spread of any of the communicable diseases from such State or possession to any other State or possession, he/she may take such measures to prevent such spread of the diseases as he/she deems reasonably necessary, including inspection. . . .

§70.5 Requirements Relating to Travelers under a Federal Order of Isolation, Quarantine, or Conditional Release.

(a) The following provisions are applicable to any individual under a Federal order of isolation, quarantine, or conditional release with regard to a quarantinable communicable disease . . . :

(1) Except as specified under the terms of a Federal conditional release order, no such individual shall travel in interstate traffic or from one State or U.S. territory to another without a written travel permit issued by the Director. . . .

(e) The Director may additionally apply the provisions in paragraph[] (a) . . . of this section to individuals traveling interstate or entirely intrastate . . . whenever the Director makes a determination under 42 CFR 70.2 that based on the existence of inadequate local control such measures are needed to prevent the spread of any of the communicable diseases from such State or U.S. territory to any other State or U.S. territory. . . .

§70.6 Apprehension and Detention of Persons with Quarantinable Communicable Diseases.

(a) The Director may authorize the apprehension, medical examination, quarantine, isolation, or conditional release of any individual for the purpose of preventing the introduction, transmission, and spread of quarantinable communicable diseases, as specified by Executive Order, based upon a finding that:

(1) The individual is reasonably believed to be infected with a quarantinable communicable disease in a qualifying stage and is moving or about to move from a State into another State; or

(2) The individual is reasonably believed to be infected with a quarantinable communicable disease in a qualifying stage and constitutes a probable source of infection to other individuals who may be moving from a State into another State. . . .

§70.10 Public Health Prevention Measures to Detect Communicable Disease.

(a) The Director may conduct public health prevention measures at U.S. airports, seaports, railway stations, bus terminals, and other locations where individuals may gather to engage in interstate travel, through non-invasive procedures determined appropriate by the Director to detect the presence of communicable diseases.

(b) As part of the public health prevention measures, the Director may require individuals to provide contact information such as U.S. and foreign addresses, telephone numbers, email addresses, and other contact information, as well as information concerning their intended destination, health status, known or possible exposure history, and travel history. . . .

§70.12 Medical Examinations.

(a) The Director may require an individual to undergo a medical examination as part of a Federal order for quarantine, isolation, or conditional release for a quarantinable communicable disease. . . .

(d) Individuals reasonably believed to be infected based on the results of a medical examination may be isolated, or if such results are inconclusive or unavailable, individuals may be quarantined or conditionally released in accordance with this part. . . .

§70.14 Requirements Relating to the Issuance of a Federal Order for Quarantine, Isolation, or Conditional Release.

(a) A Federal order authorizing quarantine, isolation, or conditional release shall be in writing, signed by the Director, and contain the following information:

(1) The identity of the individual or group subject to the order;

(2) The location of the quarantine or isolation or, in the case of conditional release, the entity to who[m] and means by which the individual shall report for public health supervision;

(3) An explanation of the factual basis underlying the Director's reasonable belief that the individual is in the qualifying stage of a quarantinable communicable disease;

(4) An explanation of the factual basis underlying the Director's reasonable belief that the individual is moving or about to move from one State into another or constitutes a probable source of infection to others who may be moving from one State into another . . . .

(b) A Federal order authorizing quarantine, isolation, or conditional release shall be served on the individual no later than 72 hours after the individual has been apprehended, except that the Federal order may be published or posted in a conspicuous location if the Federal order is applicable to a group of individuals and individual service would be impracticable. . . .

(d) Nothing in this section shall affect the constitutional or
statutory rights of individuals to obtain judicial review of their Federal
detention. . . .

[NSL p. 1236, CTL p. 864. Add this note to the Insurrection Act.]

In 2016 the Insurrection Act was renumbered by the National
Defense Authorization Act for Fiscal Year 2017, Pub. L. No. 114-328,
§1241(a)(2), 130 Stat. 2000, 2497 (2016). The correct citation is now 10
U.S.C. §§251-255 (2012 & Supp. IV 2016).

[NSL p. 1291. Add to end of Note 1.]

In June 2016, Congress enacted the FOIA Improvement Act of 2016,
Pub. L. No. 114-185, 130 Stat. 538. The act codifies the "presumption of
openness" first embraced in President Clinton's executive order on
classification, directing agencies to "withhold information . . . only if the
agency reasonably foresees that disclosure would harm an interest
protected by an exemption described in subsection (b)" or "disclosure is
prohibited by law." §2(1)(D), 130 Stat. at 539 (adding new 5 U.S.C.
§552(a)(8)(A)). It also establishes an absolute sunset of 25 years for
records withheld under Exemption 5, §2(2), 130 Stat. at 539-540
(amending 5 U.S.C. §552(b)(5)), and it further limits search fees if an
agency response is delayed. §2(1)(B), 130 Stat. at 538-539 (amending 5
U.S.C. §552(a)(4)(A)(viii)).

Section 4 of the 2016 measure, 130 Stat. at 544, additionally amends
the Federal Records Act, 44 U.S.C. §3102 (see casebook p. 1317), to
require agencies to establish "procedures for identifying records of
general interest or use to the public that are appropriate for public
disclosure, and for posting such records in a publicly accessible
electronic format."

[NSL p. 1293. Replace the last paragraph of Note 7 with the following.]

To underscore the significance of interpretations like *Goland*,
consider a court's resolution of a FOIA request for a report of the Senate
Select Committee on Intelligence on the CIA's detention and
interrogation program during the George W. Bush administration. See

casebook p. 1024. The 6,963-page full, final report was sent to the CIA and other agencies on December 10, 2014, by then-SSCI chair, Democratic Senator Dianne Feinstein, with a request that it be "made available within the CIA and other components of the Executive Branch for use as broadly as appropriate to help make sure that this experience is never repeated." Such use presumably would have made the report an "agency record." Nevertheless, each agency recipient reportedly locked its copy away without integrating it into its record system. A month later, on January 14, 2015, the new SSCI chair, Republican Senator Richard Burr, asked that all of the executive branch recipients return their copies to the committee.

Fearing destruction of the report and all electronic copies, the ACLU submitted a FOIA request for the full report. The D.C. Circuit, relying on its earlier rulings in *Goland* and other cases, denied the request based on its finding that Senate Intelligence Committee intended to retain "control" of the report. *ACLU v. CIA*, 823 F.3d 655 (D.C. Cir. 2016), *cert. denied*, 137 S. Ct. 1837 (2017). President Obama, however, sent a copy of the report to the National Archives and Records Administration, where it will be preserved as a presidential record under the Presidential Records Act (see casebook p. 1316), although it may not be made public, if ever, until at least 2029. Additional copies are reportedly held by the Pentagon and in the files of a federal district court in the District of Columbia in a habeas case involving two Guantánamo detainees. *See* Mark Mazzetti, Matthew Rosenberg & Charlie Savage, *Torture Report Could Remain Under Wraps*, N.Y. Times, June 3, 2017.

[NSL p. 1318. Add to end of Part B.1.]

Congress weighed in on this controversy in 2014. Presidential and Federal Records Act Amendments of 2014, Pub. L. No. 113-187, §2(a)(1), 128 Stat. 2003, 2003-2005 (adding new 44 U.S.C. §2208). The amendments provide that 60 days before the National Archivist releases any presidential record to the public, she must notify both the current President and the one in whose administration the record was created. 44 U.S.C. §2208(a)(1). If either claims a constitutionally based privilege against disclosure, the incumbent President (but not the former President) may block the release of the record, unless a court of last resort rules otherwise. 44 U.S.C. §2208(c), (d).

The 2014 amendments also address the conduct of official business using non-official electronic messaging accounts, like Twitter,

WhatsApp, or Gmail, by the President, Vice President, their staffs, or personnel of the Executive Office of the President or Vice President. Pub. L. No. 113-187, §2(e), 128 Stat. at 2006-2007 (adding new 44 U.S.C. §2209). Any presidential or vice presidential record sent from such an account must also be sent to an official messaging account. 44 U.S.C. §2209(a). The 2014 measure imposes the same requirement on all executive agency personnel. Pub. L. No. 113-187, §10, 128 Stat. at 2014-2015 (adding new 44 U.S.C. §2911). Such messages are thereby made subject to the same rules that govern preservation and disclosure of other government records, and the amendments do not differentiate between messages sent from nominally "official" accounts (such as @POTUS) and nominally "unofficial" accounts (such as @realdonaldtrump).

The House Committee on Oversight and Government Reform has expressed concern about reports that President Donald Trump deleted numerous tweets that likely constituted presidential records, in violation of the Presidential Records Act. Letter from Reps. Jason Chaffetz & Elijah E. Cummings to Donald F. McGahn, Counsel to the President (Mar. 8, 2017). On June 22, 2017, two public interest organizations sued to require the preservation of these and other records of presidential communications. *Citizens for Responsibility and Ethics in Washington v. Trump*, No. 17-1228 (D.D.C. filed June 22, 2017).

A separate issue, but one that has also arisen from President Trump's use of Twitter, is whether his denial of certain users' access to his tweets (by "blocking" them) constitutes viewpoint discrimination in violation of the First Amendment. A new lawsuit claims precisely that. *See Knight First Amendment Inst. v. Trump*, No. 17-5205 (S.D.N.Y. filed July 11, 2017). For a thoughtful analysis of the issue, see Eugene Volokh, *Is @RealDonaldTrump Violating the First Amendment By Blocking Some Twitter Users?*, The Volokh Conspiracy, June 6, 2017.

[NSL p. 1335. Insert at the end of Note 5.]

Dhiab v. Trump

United States Court of Appeals, District of Columbia Circuit,
Mar. 31, 2017
852 F.3d 1087

Before: ROGERS, Circuit Judge, and WILLIAMS and RANDOLPH,
Senior Circuit Judges.

RANDOLPH, Senior Circuit Judge: The government's appeal, and the
intervenors' cross-appeal, are from the district court's orders releasing
video recordings made at the United States Naval Base, Guantanamo
Bay, Cuba. The recordings are of military personnel removing a detainee
from his cell, transporting him to a medical unit, and force-feeding him
to keep him alive while he was on a hunger strike.

The government classified these recordings as "SECRET" because
disclosing them could damage the national security. The district court
decided that under the Constitution the public has a right to view the
recordings because the detainee's attorney filed some of them under seal,
at which point the recordings became part of the court's record. The
government's appeal is on the ground that the public has no such
constitutional right. . . .

I.

The case began when Abu Wa'el (Jihad) Dhiab filed a petition for
a writ of habeas corpus to prevent the government from force-feeding
him. . . .

. . . [Subsequently], Dhiab moved again for a preliminary injunction,
this time challenging particular government force-feeding practices. . . .
[T]he district court ordered the government to provide Dhiab's attorney,
who had been given a security clearance, copies of the video recordings,
the existence of which the government had disclosed. After the
government complied with the order, to which it objected, Dhiab's
attorney filed some of the recordings under seal.

The government recorded Dhiab's removal from his cell and his
force-feeding in order to train military guards about how to handle
detainees in such circumstances. In classifying each recording as

"SECRET," we shall assume that the government complied with Executive Order No. 13,526, 75 Fed. Reg. 707 (Dec. 29, 2009).[3] . . .

Press organizations — sixteen of them — sought to intervene in Dhiab's habeas case and asked the district court to unseal the recordings Dhiab's attorney had filed. Their motion asserted that under the First Amendment, and common law, the public had a right to see these recordings because the recordings had become part of the record of Dhiab's habeas corpus proceeding. The government did not oppose their intervention motion but it did oppose the organizations' motion to unseal the recordings. . . .

II.

The intervenors' claim that the Constitution requires this national security information, properly classified as "SECRET," to be divulged to the world because a lawyer representing a Guantanamo detainee filed some of the recordings under seal in his client's now-moot habeas corpus action is untenable. It is important to bear in mind that the Constitution gives "the President as head of the Executive Branch and as Commander in Chief" the "authority to classify and control access to information bearing on national security. . . ." [*Dep't of Navy v. Egan*, 484 U.S. 518, 527-28 (1988),] at 527. . . .

Here the government established that the recordings of Dhiab were properly classified as "SECRET." The district court did not rule otherwise, and the intervenors did not claim, let alone show, that the classifications were improper. The government submitted declarations . . . demonstrating the harm that would result from releasing any of these recordings, redacted or not.

Yet the intervenors insist that under the First Amendment, classified information submitted under seal in a judicial proceeding becomes fair game for a judicial disclosure order, such as the one the district court issued in this case. Neither the First Amendment nor any other provision of the Constitution stands for such a principle.

The intervenors rely heavily on *Press-Enterprise Co. v. Superior Court*, 478 U.S. 1, 8-9 (1986). This *Press-Enterprise II* decision will not bear the weight they place on it. The Supreme Court framed the question in *Press-Enterprise II* this way: whether the public had "a First

---

3. The intervenors did not claim, let alone establish, that the classification of the recordings was improper. The district court expressed no opinion on the subject.

Amendment right of access to the transcript of a preliminary hearing growing out of a criminal prosecution." *Id.* at 3. The Court put the question in terms of the public's right because the "First Amendment generally grants the press no right to information about a trial superior to that of the general public." *Nixon v. Warner Commc'ns, Inc.*, 435 U.S. 589 (1978).

Press-Enterprise II discovered a constitutional right in the public, although it was a qualified one: such proceedings may be sealed but only if "specific, on the record findings are made demonstrating that 'closure is essential to preserve higher values and is narrowly tailored to serve that interest.'" 478 U.S. at 13-14. . . .

Press-Enterprise II is not comparable to this case. Two differences are immediately apparent. When the Court wrote of the importance of public access to evidentiary proceedings it could not possibly have had in mind classified national security information. The case came up from a California state court. . . . The sealed record in *Press-Enterprise II* consisted of testimony and exhibits relating to murder charges, not classified material. *Id.* at 4.

The second difference is just as obvious. Unlike Dhiab's case, which was civil in nature,[8] the underlying action in *Press-Enterprise II* was a criminal prosecution. When it comes to classified national security information the Supreme Court has decided that the distinction makes a difference. *See United States v. Reynolds*, 345 U.S. 1, 12 (1953). In criminal cases, the government initiates the prosecution. Access and disclosure rights in criminal cases "do not endanger the government's paramount interest in national security. The government's interest can be protected by dismissal of the prosecution or less drastic concessions by the government in a criminal case." Bruce E. Fein, *Access to Classified Information: Constitutional and Statutory Dimensions*, 26 Wm. & Mary L. Rev. 805, 828 (1985).[9] Matters are quite different in civil cases: "the Government is not the moving party, but is a defendant. . . ." *Reynolds*, 345 U.S. at 12. For this reason, the Court in *Reynolds* held that the rationale

---

8. *See, e.g., Fay v. Noia*, 372 U.S. 391, 423 (1963), deciding that the writ of habeas corpus is a "civil remedy for the enforcement of the right to personal liberty" not "a stage of" a criminal proceeding.

9. The Classified Information Procedures Act, 18 U.S.C. app. 3, (CIPA) governs the handling of classified evidence in criminal proceedings. CIPA was enacted to limit the practice of criminal defendants threatening to disclose classified information in order to force the government to dismiss the charges. . . . [See casebook p. 1124.]

behind access to national security information in criminal cases had "no application in a civil forum." *Id.*[10] . . .

There are additional reasons why *Press-Enterprise II* does not apply to this case. To reach its result, the Supreme Court recounted the English tradition of public criminal trials, beginning — the Court wrote — before the Norman conquest. *Press-Enterprise II*, 478 U.S. at 8. Although the Court did not say as much, the idea apparently was that the Framers of the First Amendment must have had this history in the back of their collective minds. . . .

In habeas corpus cases, there is no tradition of public access comparable to that recounted in *Press-Enterprise II* with respect to criminal trials. Habeas corpus proceedings do not involve juries. Since the beginning they have been decided by judges. Early English courts were in session for only a few months each year. Paul D. Halliday, Habeas Corpus: From England to Empire 355 n.79 (2010). Yet from the fifteenth to eighteenth century, English courts regularly adjudicated habeas petitions between sessions. *Id.* at 56-57. At such times the English judges required jailers to make their returns to the writ to the judge's private chambers or to the judge's home. *Id.* at 54. The judge then made his habeas decision in private. *Id.* Between 1500 and 1800, about one-fifth of the writs the judges of England issued required the jailer make the return to chambers. *Id.* Although English judges more frequently requested returns to chambers during the vacations, the practice also occurred during terms of court. *Id.* The Habeas Corpus Act of 1679, which Blackstone described as the bulwark of English liberties, 1 William Blackstone, Commentaries on the Laws of England 133 (1765), expressly authorized the courts to issue writs of habeas corpus during vacations, thus continuing this longstanding practice. 31 Car. 2 c. 2.

Of course in this country, proceedings in open court are the norm, although there are well-established exceptions. *See, e.g., In re Motions of Dow Jones & Co.*, 142 F.3d at 502-05. But of importance here is not just the absence of any "unbroken, uncontradicted history" of public attendance at habeas corpus proceedings in eighteenth-century England. *Richmond Newspapers*, 448 U.S. at 573 (Burger, C.J., plurality opinion).

---

10. We also have recognized the difference between criminal and civil proceedings: "Neither the Supreme Court nor this Court has applied the [First Amendment right of access] outside the context of criminal judicial proceedings or the transcripts of such proceedings." *Ctr. for Nat'l Sec. Studies v. U.S. Dep't of Justice*, 331 F.3d 918, 935 (D.C. Cir. 2003).

More significant is that from the beginning of the republic to the present day, there is no tradition of publicizing secret national security information involved in civil cases, or for that matter, in criminal cases. The tradition is exactly the opposite.[15] . . .

Add to *United States v. Reynolds*, already mentioned, the case of *Totten v. United States*, 92 U.S. 105 (1875). Both of these civil cases are well-known instances in the long history of protecting national security secrets of the United States. *Reynolds* held that in a suit against the government, the plaintiff had no right to discover military or state secrets; the privilege against revealing such information was, the Court wrote, "well established." 345 U.S. at 6-7. . . .

In *Boumediene v. Bush*, the case establishing the right of Guantanamo detainees to bring habeas actions, the Court thought the unique proceedings it was authorizing might risk "widespread dissemination of classified information." 553 U.S. 723, 796 (2008). To guard against this the Court wrote that the government "has a legitimate interest in protecting sources and methods of intelligence gathering; and we expect that the District Court will use its discretion to accommodate this interest to the greatest extent possible." *Boumediene*, 553 U.S. at 796.

To that end, Guantanamo habeas proceedings have been litigated under orders designed to protect classified information. *See, e.g., In re Guantanamo Bay Detainee Litig.*, 577 F. Supp. 2d 143 (D.D.C. 2008). These protective orders require not only that classified information be maintained under seal, but also that counsel (with a security clearance) not disclose classified information at any hearing or proceeding. *Id.* at 150, 153. The government informs us that Guantanamo habeas cases routinely involve closed sessions to protect classified information from the public eye. Dhiab's case is no exception: in his habeas proceedings, the district court held an evidentiary hearing from which the public was excluded. *Id.* at 21.

As against this, the intervenors are unable to cite a single case in which a court — other than the district court here — found that the First Amendment compelled public disclosure of properly classified national security information in a habeas proceeding, or in any other type of civil proceeding.

---

15. *See, e.g., McGehee v. Casey*, 718 F.2d 1137, 1147 (D.C. Cir. 1983): "As a general rule, citizens have no first amendment right of access to traditionally nonpublic government information. . . ."

Press-Enterprise II spoke of a need to take into account "experience and logic" in determining whether the First Amendment required a record of a judicial proceeding to be released to the world. 478 U.S. at 9. The "experience" in habeas corpus cases and in cases involving classified documents have already been discussed.

As to "logic," it is important to remember that logic does not give starting points. First principles do. For this case the starting point was established at the Founding. The preamble to the Constitution gives equal billing to the national defense and "the Blessings of Liberty." U.S. Const. pmbl. As the Supreme Court stated, there is no higher value than the security of the nation, a value the Court deemed a "compelling interest." *Haig v. Agee*, 453 U.S. 280, 307 (1981) (internal quotation omitted).

Press-Enterprise II therefore does not apply to this case and neither the intervenors nor the public at large have a right under the First Amendment to receive properly classified national security information filed in court during the pendency of Dhiab's petition for a writ of habeas corpus.

III.

Even if the intervenors had a qualified First Amendment right of access to the Dhiab recordings, we would still reverse the district court's decision. The court's ruling that the government failed to show a "substantial probability" of harm to a higher value was clear error. *Press-Enterprise II*, 478 U.S. at 14 (internal quotation omitted).

The government identified multiple ways in which unsealing these recordings would likely impair national security. Two of these risks — detainees triggering forcible encounters and developing countermeasures — together and individually, were enough to prevent these recordings from becoming public. The government's declarations explained that the recordings would enable detainees, assisted by outside militants, to develop countermeasures to the guards' cell-extraction and enteral-feeding techniques. . . .

. . . Information gleaned from the recordings could reach current detainees, who communicate with family members and other outside persons and have some access to outside media. Militants could also use the recordings to train fighters the government may capture and detain in the future. When detainees resist what are already hazardous procedures for the guards, this could further endanger government personnel at Guantanamo. Guards have been kicked, grabbed, punched, knocked down, bitten, and sprayed with bodily fluids. The government's interest in ensuring safe and secure military operations clearly overcomes any qualified First Amendment right of access. . . .

The government also explained in detail the risk that extremists would use the recordings to incite violence against American troops abroad and as propaganda to recruit fighters. The recordings are "particularly subject to use" because they depict "a forcible interaction between . . . personnel and the detainees." Declaration of Rear Admiral Sinclair M. Harris, ¶12. Images are more provocative than written or verbal descriptions. Extremists have used Guantanamo Bay imagery in their propaganda and in carrying out attacks on Americans. *Id.* ¶¶8,10. For example, the Islamic State beheaded American journalists wearing orange jumpsuits commonly associated with Guantanamo Bay detainees. *Id.* ¶8. In his forced final statement before his execution, Steven Sotloff, one of the journalists, was forced to mention the continued operation of Guantanamo as a reason why he was about to be murdered. *Id.*

. . . [T]he government unquestionably can classify documents based on the risk our enemies will use them to incite violence. *Judicial Watch, Inc. v. United States Department of Defense*, 715 F.3d 937, 943 (D.C. Cir. 2013), so held.

It bears repeating that the government "has a *compelling* interest in protecting . . . the secrecy of information important to our national security. . . ." *McGehee*, 718 F.2d at 1143 (*quoting Snepp v. United States*, 444 U.S. at 509 n.3 (per curiam) (emphasis and alteration in original)). The district court did not disagree with the "SECRET" classification of these recordings, and neither did the intervenors. By definition, "the unauthorized disclosure of [the recordings] reasonably could be expected to cause serious damage to the national security." Executive Order No. 13,526 §1.2 (a)(2). . . .

The district court did not reach the intervenors' common-law claim because it ruled in their favor on the basis of the First Amendment. *Dhiab*, 70 F. Supp. 3d at 492 n.2; *see Nixon v. Warner Commc'ns, Inc.*, 435 U.S. at 598-99. The law of this circuit is that the need to "guard against risks to national security interests" overcomes a common-law claim for access. *United States v. Hubbard*, 650 F.2d 293, 315-16 (D.C. Cir. 1980). Because keeping the recordings sealed is narrowly tailored to protect the government's compelling interest in guarding national security, intervenors cannot prevail on their common-law claim. . . .

Reversed.

ROGERS, Circuit Judge, concurring in part and concurring in the judgment. . . . I would apply the experience and logic analysis of *Press-Enterprise Co. v. Superior Court*, 478 U.S. 1, 8-9 (1986) ("*Press-Enterprise II*"), and so my conclusion about when the government's interest in protecting information classified as SECRET will outweigh the public's First Amendment interest is more tentative than Judge Randolph's. At the same time, I tend to be less tentative than my colleagues about the nature of the historical background and the level of generality properly used in the analysis. . . .

Although neither the Supreme Court nor this court has applied the qualified First Amendment right of access to judicial civil proceedings, in *Press-Enterprise II*, the Supreme Court explained that the access right extends to any judicial proceeding where there is a "tradition of accessibility" and "public access plays a significant positive role in the functioning of the particular process in question." 478 U.S. at 8. The First Amendment guarantees the "rights to speak and to publish concerning what takes place at a trial." *Richmond Newspapers, Inc. v. Virginia*, 448 U.S. 555, 576-77 (1980). The then-Chief Justice stated that "[w]hether the public has a right to attend trials of civil cases is a question not raised by this case, but we note that historically both civil and criminal trials have been presumptively open." *Id.* at 580 n.17. By its terms, the experience and logic test does not limit the right of access to criminal proceedings. Every circuit to consider the issue has concluded that the qualified First Amendment right of public access applies to civil as well as criminal proceedings. . . .

The Supreme Court has not required there be a history of absolute accessibility to satisfy the "experience" prong; a "*near* uniform practice of state and federal courts" suffices. *Press-Enterprise II*, 478 U.S. at 10 (emphasis added). There can be "gaps." . . . Nonetheless, in relying on English history from the 16th to 18th centuries, my colleagues appear unpersuaded, surprisingly, that the overwhelming practice of open habeas corpus proceedings — at least 80% — establishes a sufficient tradition of accessibility. . . . [T]here was a well-settled expectation that habeas proceedings would be open to the public when the courts were in session. . . .

The qualified First Amendment right of access fits well with the privilege of habeas corpus, which was originally "one of the few safeguards of liberty specified in [the] Constitution." [*Boumediene v. Bush*, 553 U.S. 723 (2008),] at 739. Because criminal trials and habeas proceedings are designed to protect against abuses of Executive power and guard individual liberty, why would the First Amendment right of access apply differently in the two proceedings? . . . The qualified right of public access plays a significant positive role in criminal proceedings by ensuring that "standards of fairness are being observed." *Press-Enterprise Co. v. Superior Court*, 464 U.S. 501, 508 (1984). In habeas proceedings, the absence of a jury, "long recognized as an inestimable safeguard against the corrupt or overzealous prosecutor and against the complaint, biased or eccentric judge [,] makes the importance of public access . . . significant." *Press-Enterprise II*, 478 U.S. at 12–13. Also, "[t]o the extent the First Amendment embraces a right of access to criminal trials, it is to ensure that th[e] constitutionally protected discussion of governmental affairs is an informed one." *Globe Newspaper Co. v. Superior Court*, 457 U.S. 596, 604-05 (1982) (internal quotation marks omitted). Because the writ of habeas corpus is an important part of our Constitution and a "vital instrument for the protection of individual liberty," *Boumediene*, 553 U.S. at 743, the public's qualified right to informed discussion about its government would apply no less in these proceedings.

Nor is there reason to conclude that when the Supreme Court articulated the experience and logic test, "it could not possibly have had in mind classified national security information." Op. at —— (Randolph, J.). The Court's test protects against threats to our nation's security by prohibiting disclosure when it will cause a "substantial probability" of harm to an "overriding interest." *Press-Enterprise II*, 478 U.S. at 7, 14. The . . . Court is well aware that First Amendment rights will often clash with national security concerns, *see, e.g.*, *Dennis et al. v. United States*, 341 U.S. 494 (1951). Yet the Court crafted a test where the threshold First Amendment question is whether "the particular process in question" passes the experience and logic test, *Press-Enterprise II*, 478 U.S. at 8, not whether the records submitted in that proceeding contain classified information. Because the test accounts for the protection of national security information, the presence of such information in a judicial proceeding does not crowd out the decades-old and flexible approach set forth in *Press-Enterprise II*.

[The opinion of WILLIAMS, Senior Circuit Judge, concurring in part and concurring in the judgment, is omitted.]

—————————————

Note that neither Judge Rogers nor Judge Williams joined in Part II of Judge Randolph's opinion — wherein he concluded that there is no qualified First Amendment right of public access to habeas proceedings, including (but presumably not limited to) the Guantánamo detainee litigation. Thus, that issue remains at least nominally open within the D.C. Circuit.

And as one of us has argued, if and when the issue arises again, "it will be crucial . . . to recognize that (1) there's no controlling opinion in *Dhiab* on whether there even is a qualified First Amendment right of public access to such proceedings; and (2) as a matter of first impression, there are compelling reasons why there should be — even if it can and should be overcome in individual cases." Steve Vladeck, *The D.C. Circuit Gives Short Shrift to Public Access to Guantánamo Proceedings*, Just Security, Apr. 10, 2017.

[NSL p. 1381. Insert at the end of C. "AUTHORIZED" LEAKS.]

More recently, President Donald Trump reportedly shared extremely sensitive intelligence with Russian officials during an Oval Office meeting, violating an agreement with an ally that furnished the information, and possibly jeopardizing a critical source within the Islamic State. The information, which was withheld from the public at the government's insistence, reportedly concerned a terrorist threat related to laptop computers on airplanes, as well as U.S. counter-measures. *See* Greg Miller & Greg Jaffe, *Trump Revealed Highly Classified Information to Russian Foreign Minister and Ambassador*, Wash. Post, May 15, 2017. A dispute immediately arose about whether the President had acted illegally. *See, e.g.*, Matt Zapotosky, *No, Trump Did Not Break the Law in Talking Classified Details with the Russians*, Wash. Post, May 16, 2017; Elizabeth Goitein, *Don't Be So Quick to Call Those Disclosures "Legal,"* Just Security, May 17, 2017. Can you marshal arguments for and against the legality of President Trump's (apparently unplanned) disclosures?

Some aspects of "authorized" leaks are analyzed in Jennifer Elsea, *The Protection of Classified Information: The Legal Framework* 16-19 (Cong. Res. Serv. RS21900), May 18, 2017.

[CTL p. 925. Insert at the end of Note 2.]

Many banks have responded to sanctions regimes, and to anti-money laundering and anti-terror financing regulations, by "derisking": terminating or restricting business relations to avoid rather than just manage risk. *See* Sue E. Eckert with Kay Guinane & Andrea Hall, *Financial Access for U.S. Nonprofits* (Feb. 2017), at v. A 2015 survey of U.S. nonprofit organizations working abroad indicated that such derisking significantly impacts the access of such organizations to funding needed for humanitarian activities, while arguably "increas[ing] the risk of illicit finance" through more opaque harder-to-regulate channels. *Id.* at viii-ix. *See also* Jayne Huckerby et al. (Duke International Human Rights Clinic and Women Peacemakers Program), *Tightening the Pursestrings: What Countering Terrorism Financing Costs Gender Equality and Security* (Mar. 2017); Rob Kuznia, *Scrutiny over Terrorism Funding Hampers Charitable Work in Ravaged Countries,* Wash. Post, Apr. 19, 2017. Suppose, however, that the "humanitarian activity" is conducted by an FTO like Hamas, legitimating the FTO politically and helping it to recruit candidates for terrorism? *See Holder v. Humanitarian Law Proj.*, 561 U.S. 1, 30-31 (2010) (CTL p. 702) (quoting government affidavit stating that "some designated . . . [FTOs] use social and political components to recruit personnel to carry out terrorist operations, and to provide support to criminal terrorists and their families in aid of such operations"); *Boim v. Holy Land Found. for Relief & Dev.* ("*Boim III*"), 549 F.3d 685, 698 (7th Cir. 2008) (en banc) (CTL p. 934) ("Hamas's social welfare activities reinforce its terrorist activities . . . .").

[CTL p. 927. Insert after the first sentence of Part A.]

On Sept. 26, 2016, Congress overrode President's Obama's veto to pass the Justice Against Sponsors of Terrorism Act (JASTA), Pub. L. No. 114-222, 130 Stat. 852, adding §2333(d) to the ATA and eliminating the defense of sovereign immunity for certain claims against state sovereigns arising out of acts of international terrorism. The possible impact of JASTA on civil claims is addressed *infra* in this *Supplement*.

[CTL p. 928. Insert after §2333(a) in the boxed material.]

(d) (1) In this subsection, the term "person" has the meaning given the term in section 1 of title 1.

(2) In an action under subsection (a) for an injury arising from an act of international terrorism committed, planned, or authorized by an

organization that had been designated as a foreign terrorist organization under section 219 of the Immigration and Nationality Act (8 U.S.C. 1189), as of the date on which such act of international terrorism was committed, planned, or authorized, liability may be asserted as to any person who aids and abets, by knowingly providing substantial assistance, or who conspires with the person who committed such an act of international terrorism.

[CTL p. 937. Insert at the end of Note 3.]

By enacting §2333(d), Congress has now expressly created statutory secondary liability against defendants who aid and abet or conspire with "persons" (defined broadly to include organizations) who commit acts of international terrorism "committed, planned or authorized" by a designated foreign terrorist organization. Had this provision been enacted before the terrorist act that killed Boim, would it have authorized claims against the defendants in the *Boim* litigation? Does it now encompass *all* ATA claims against secondary defendants, or are there still some possible secondary defendants that fall beyond its scope? If so, does it preclude claims against the latter; that is, is the secondary liability that it authorizes exclusive? *See* JASTA §2(b) (stating that the purpose of adding §2333(d) was "to provide civil litigants with the broadest possible basis, consistent with the Constitution of the United States, to seek relief against persons, entities, and foreign countries, wherever acting and wherever they may be found, that have provided material support, directly or indirectly, to foreign organizations or persons that engage in terrorist activities against the United States."). Note that JASTA is otherwise unclear about the theory of liability upon which foreign sovereign defendants (who cannot be sued under the ATA, *see* 28 U.S.C. §2337(2)) may be held liable under non-ATA causes of action. *See* JASTA §3(a) (codified at 28 U.S.C. §1605B(b)).

[CTL p. 937. Insert at the end of Note 4.]

In enacting JASTA, Congress found that the D.C. Circuit's decision in *Halberstam v. Welch*, 705 F.2d 472 (D.C. Cir. 1972), "provides the proper legal framework for how [aiding-and-abetting and conspiracy liability] shall function" under the terrorism chapter of the federal criminal laws. JASTA §2(a)(5). In *Halberstam*, the court of appeals affirmed the civil aiding-and-abetting liability of the live-in companion of a cat burglar for his murder of a homeowner during a burglary, even though she had only performed accounting services for the burglar and neither intended, nor even knew, that he would commit the murder. It was enough that she had a "general awareness" of his unlawful activity of burglary, provided "substantial assistance" to him by her services, and could reasonably foresee the risk of violence posed by his nighttime burglaries. Thus, §2333(d) liability does not require proof of a defendant's intent to commit a terrorist act.

[CTL p. 938. Insert at the end of Note 5.]

Section 2333(d) liability does not require proof of strict "but for" or "tracing" causation either. In *Halberstam, supra* (which supplies the controlling legal framework for §2333(d) liability), the court of appeals found that it was enough for aiding-and-abetting or conspiracy liability that the underlying tort was reasonably foreseeable. If anything, *Halberstam* seems to set out a more lenient causation requirement than *Rothstein*.

[CTL p. 939. Insert at the end of the third paragraph of Note 8.]

The Supreme Court has granted certiorari in *In re Arab Bank, PLC Alien Tort Statute Litigation*, 808 F.3d 144 (2d Cir. 2015), *cert. granted sub nom. Jesner v. Arab Bank*, 137 S. Ct. 1432 (Apr. 3, 2017) (No. 16-499), on the question, "Whether a corporation may be named as a defendant in a federal common-law action brought under the Alien Tort Statute, 28 U.S.C. 1350." The Solicitor General of the United States has argued that the answer is yes, although it has also urged remand for the court of appeals to consider extraterritoriality, as noted below. *See* Brief for the United States As *Amicus Curiae* Supporting Neither Party, *Jesner*, No. 16-499.

[CTL p. 940. Insert at the end of Note 9.]

In *Jesner, supra*, the Acting Solicitor General urged the Supreme Court to remand for the court of appeals to consider whether the dollar-clearing activities in the United States of a Jordanian bank charged with funding terrorism in Israel sufficiently "touches and concerns" the United States to support application of the ATS to the bank's activities. Brief for the United States As *Amicus Curiae* Supporting Neither Party at 25-30, *Jesner v. Arab Bank, PLC*, 137 S. Ct. 1432 (Apr. 3, 2017) (No. 16-499) (mem.). Note that, as relevant to that issue, a different cert. petition has asked the Supreme Court to resolve the (now five-way) circuit split over the scope of the ATS's extraterritorial application after and in light of *Kiobel. See* Petition for a Writ of Certiorari, *Adhikari v. Kellogg Brown & Root, Inc.*, No. 16-1461 (U.S. filed June 2, 2017).

[CTL p. 953. Insert at the end of the page.]

The most recent — and high-profile — example of the many doctrinal and normative tensions described in this section (and this chapter) is Congress's enactment on September 28, 2016, over President Obama's veto, of the Justice Against Sponsors of Terrorism Act (JASTA), Pub. L. No. 114-222, 130 Stat. 852. JASTA was passed against the backdrop of efforts by the families of 9/11 victims to pursue claims against Saudi Arabia, based upon their belief that the Saudi government (or senior officials therein) helped to finance Al Qaeda in the run-up to the attacks. Because the executive branch does not recognize Saudi Arabia as a "state sponsor of terrorism," the route surveyed in Section B of this chapter was unavailable.

Instead, the families initially tried to sue Saudi Arabia under a different exception to the FSIA — for "noncommercial torts" — only to run into a series of procedural and substantive obstacles that prevented courts from reaching the merits of their claims. *See generally In re Terrorist Attacks on September 11, 2001*, 134 F. Supp. 3d 774, 778-779 (S.D.N.Y. 2015) (summarizing the background). As one of us has explained, as initially conceived, JASTA would have simply cleared away those obstacles by eliminating foreign sovereign immunity in any case in which a foreign sovereign (whether a "state sponsor of terrorism" or not) was directly or indirectly responsible for an act of "international terrorism" committed by a "designated foreign terrorist organization" on U.S. soil, even if the foreign sovereign's conduct took place wholly overseas. *See* Steve Vladeck, *The 9/11 Civil Litigation and the Justice Against Sponsors of Terrorism Act (JASTA)*, Just Security, Apr. 18, 2016.

But in clearing away those obstacles, the bill Congress actually passed (in marked contrast to the original version) created three others:

First, JASTA creates a formal procedure allowing the U.S. government to intervene in cases asserting "JASTA claims" for the purpose of seeking a stay "if the Secretary of State certifies that the United States is engaged in good faith discussions with the foreign state defendant concerning the resolution of the claims against the foreign state." JASTA §5(c)(1). Although the stay only lasts 180 days, *see id.* §5(c)(2)(A), it is renewable (in perpetuity). *Id.* §5(c)(2)(B)(ii).

Second, in contrast to the original bill, JASTA as enacted is silent as to whether a foreign sovereign defendant can be held liable based upon theories of secondary liability, per the discussion at casebook pp. 936-937. Indeed, although Section 4 of JASTA expressly authorizes aiding-and-abetting liability for "JASTA claims" under the Anti-Terrorism Act, JASTA does not repeal the ATA's ban on suits against foreign sovereigns, *see* 18 U.S.C. §2337(2), and it is otherwise silent on secondary liability for common-law tort claims under the FSIA. *See* JASTA §3(b). Thus, JASTA may dramatically expand the class of claims plaintiffs can pursue against *private* defendants, but it appears to keep the law under the FSIA (for suits against foreign sovereign defendants) largely as Congress found it.

Third, and perhaps most significantly, JASTA as enacted does not appear to allow for the *enforcement* of judgments arising out of "JASTA claims" against foreign sovereign defendants, because it leaves untouched 28 U.S.C. §1610, the FSIA provision that outlines the circumstances in which federal courts are allowed to attach or otherwise seize foreign sovereign assets located within the United States for the purpose of satisfying judgments obtained under the FSIA. Although the original bill would simply have folded "JASTA claims" into the existing state-sponsor-of-terrorism exception codified at 28 U.S.C. §1605A (for which attachment and execution are already authorized by 28 U.S.C. §1610(a)(7) and (b)(3)), JASTA as enacted creates a brand-new exception to foreign sovereign immunity (28 U.S.C. §1605B), with no corresponding exception to immunity from attachment or execution in §1610. Thus, the best that JASTA plaintiffs can hope for in suits against a foreign sovereign — assuming that they can overcome the first two obstacles outlined above — appears to be an unenforceable judgment.

In his veto message, President Obama emphasized JASTA's significant costs to U.S. foreign policy in general, and to the United States' complicated relationship with Saudi Arabia, in particular, along with the concern that Congress's weakening of foreign sovereign immunity could entice other countries to do the same vis-a-vis claims against the United States. *See The White House, Veto Message from the*

President — S. 2040, Sept. 23, 2016. It is certainly a fair question
whether the benefits of the original bill would have outweighed the costs.
But given how much those benefits were reduced in the final version, is
it not fair to claim, as one of us has, that JASTA is "the worst of all
worlds"? Jack Goldsmith & Stephen I. Vladeck, *Why Obama Should
Veto 9/11 Families Bill*, CNN.com, Sept. 13, 2016. Leaving aside its
impact on suits against private defendants, how, if at all, would you have
modified the FSIA in light of this note and the materials discussed in this
chapter?